ECDL Module 4:
Spreadsheets

Springer

London
Berlin
Heidelberg
New York
Barcelona
Hong Kong
Milan
Paris
Singapore
Tokyo

ECDL Module 4: Spreadsheets

ECDL – the European PC standard

by **David Stott**

Springer

BCS

The Publisher and the BCS would like to publicly acknowledge the vital support of the ECDL Foundation in validating and approving this book for the purpose of studying for the European-wide ECDL qualification.

Springer-Verlag London Ltd, Sweetapple House, Catteshall Road, Godalming, Surrey GU7 3DJ or

The British Computer Society, 1 Sanford Street, Swindon, Wiltshire SN1 1HJ

ISBN 1-85233-445-2

British Library Cataloguing in Publication Data
Stott, David
    ECDL module 4: spreadsheets: ECDL – the European PC standard. – (European computer driving licence)
    1. Microsoft Excel 97 (Computer file)
    I. Title
    005.3'69

    ISBN 1852334452

Printed and bound at The Cromwell Press, Trowbridge, Wiltshire, England.
34/3830-543210 Printed on acid-free paper SPIN 10792510

Preface

This book is intended to help you successfully complete the test for
Module 4 of the European Computer Driving Licence (ECDL). However
before we start working through the actual content of the guide you
may find it useful to know a little bit more about the ECDL in general
and where this particular Module fits into the overall framework.

What Is The ECDL?

The European Computer Driving Licence (ECDL) is a European-wide
qualification that enables people to demonstrate their competence in
computer skills. It certifies the candidate's knowledge and competence
in personal computer usage at a basic level and is based upon a single
agreed syllabus.

This syllabus covers a range of specific knowledge areas and skill sets,
which are broken down into seven modules. Each of the modules
must be passed before the ECDL certificate can be awarded, though
they may be taken in any order but must be completed within a three
year period.

Testing of candidates is at audited testing centres, and successful
completion of the test will demonstrate the holder's basic knowledge
and competence in using a personal computer and common computer
applications.

The implementation of the ECDL in the UK is being managed by the
British Computer Society. It is growing at a tremendous rate and is set
to become the most widely recognised qualification in the field of
work-related computer use.

The ECDL Modules

The seven modules which make up the ECDL certificate are described
briefly below:

Module 1: Basic Concepts of Information Technology covers the
physical make-up of a personal computer and some of the basic
concepts of Information Technology such as data storage and memory,
and the uses of information networks within computing. It also looks
at the application of computer software in society and the use of IT
systems in everyday situations. Some basic security and legal issues are
also addressed.

Module 2: Using the Computer and Managing Files covers the basic functions of a personal computer and its operating system. In particular it looks at operating effectively within the desktop environment, managing and organising files and directories, and working with desktop icons.

Module 3: Word Processing covers the use of a word processing application on a personal computer. It looks at the basic operations associated with creating, formatting and finishing a word processing document ready for distribution. It also addresses some of the more advanced features such as creating standard tables, using pictures and images within a document, importing objects and using mail merge tools.

Module 4: Spreadsheets covers the basic concepts of spreadsheets and the ability to use a spreadsheet application on a personal computer. Included are the basic operations for developing, formatting and using a spreadsheet, together with the use of basic formulas and functions to carry out standard mathematical and logical operations. Importing objects and creating graphs and charts are also covered.

Module 5: Database covers the basic concepts of databases and the ability to use a database on a personal computer. It addresses the design and planning of a simple database, and the retrieval of information from a database through the use of query, select and sort tools.

Module 6: Presentation covers the use of presentation tools on a personal computer, in particular creating, formatting and preparing presentations. The requirement to create a variety of presentations for different audiences and situations is also addressed.

Module 7: Information and Communication is divided into two main sections, the first of which covers basic Web search tasks using a Web browser and search engine tools. The second section addresses the use of electronic mail software to send and receive messages, to attach documents, and to organise and manage message folders and directories.

This guide focuses upon Module 4.

How To Use This Guide

The purpose of this guide is to take you through all of the knowledge areas and skill sets specified in the syllabus for Module 4. The use of clear, non technical explanations and self paced exercises will provide you with an understanding of the key elements of the syllabus and give you a solid foundation for moving on to take the ECDL test relating to this Module. All exercises contained within this guide are based upon the Windows 98 operating system and Office 97 software.

Each chapter has a well defined set of objectives that relate directly to the syllabus for the ECDL Module 4. Because the guide is structured in a logical sequence you are advised to work through the chapters one at a time from the beginning. Throughout each chapter there are various review questions so that you can determine whether you have understood the principles involved correctly prior to moving on to the next step.

Conventions Used In This Guide

Throughout this guide you will come across notes alongside a number of icons. They are all designed to provide you with specific information related to the section of the book you are currently working through. The icons and the particular types of information they relate to are as follows:

Additional Information: Further information or explanation about a specific point.

Caution: A word of warning about the risks associated with a particular action, together with guidance, where necessary on how to avoid any pitfalls.

Definition: A plain English definition of a newly introduced term or concept.

Short Cuts: Short cuts and hints for using a particular program more effectively.

As you are working through the various exercises contained within this guide, you will be asked to carry out a variety of actions:

● Where we refer to commands or items that you are required to select from the PC screen, then we indicate these in bold, for example: Click on the **Yes** button.
● Where you are asked to key text in to the PC, then we indicate this in italics, for example: Type in the words '*Saving my work*'.

You should now be in a position to use this guide, so lets get started. Good luck!

Contents

Introduction

This module of the BCS training course for ECDL qualification is concerned with the subject of Spreadsheet applications and is based on Microsoft's Excel 97 software.

Before embarking on the task of learning how to use Excel it is important to understand what Spreadsheet packages are and what role they play in modern PC based computing.

Definition: The modern spreadsheet package is a tool that can be used to create, edit, modify, process, and display information in tabular form. Essentially this means data that is normally arranged in rows and columns, as for example in an accounting ledger. However, spreadsheet software is not only suitable for dealing with accounting data and can be used for practically any task that involves the need to process numbers or perform calculations.

Like most other spreadsheet packages, Excel is based on the principle of providing the user with a very large 'virtual' sheet of paper on which to record and manipulate information on-screen. This concept of using a large sheet of paper is a fundamental aspect of the typical spreadsheet package and if you were to compare Excel's virtual spreadsheet to a physical piece of paper, then the paper would be approximately 5 metres wide and 325 metres long! Computer spreadsheets are generally divided up into rows and columns in the form of a grid of small rectangles called 'cells', where data is recorded. However, the primary feature of the spreadsheet is its ability to perform calculations on the data stored in cells and once 'programmed' a spreadsheet can update itself automatically.

Most modern windows based spreadsheet packages like Excel provide extensive formatting facilities so that data doesn't have to appear in rather plain looking tables. Using these facilities it is possible to produce spreadsheets with a much more attractive and professional looking appearance. In addition, Excel can also be used to process raw data and present it in a pictorial form such as charts and graphs.

Microsoft Excel 97 has many important features which make it suitable for performing a wide variety of data processing tasks and we shall cover a number of these in this module. Using Excel you can perform the following tasks:

● Create, edit and save spreadsheets.
● Modify existing spreadsheets.
● Publish spreadsheet data on Internet web pages.
● Create spreadsheets containing text, charts, images, audio, and video.
● Copy, move, delete, or rearrange spreadsheets within main spreadsheet files called Workbooks.
● Copy, move, delete, or rearrange data stored in areas of a spreadsheet.
● Perform various calculations on data held in spreadsheets.
● Sort spreadsheet data into ascending or descending order.
● Modify and format text and numerical data.
● Modify and format cells, rows, and columns.
● Incorporate information from other packages into spreadsheets.
● Print whole of parts of spreadsheets in various formats.
● Generate graphs and charts based on spreadsheet data.

This guide is structured in chapters that are designed to be followed in a logical sequence, therefore you are advised to work through the guide one chapter at a time from the beginning. At the end of each chapter there are some review questions so that you can determine whether you have understood the principles involved correctly.

Getting Started

In this chapter you will learn how to

- *Open and close a spreadsheet application.*
- *Make modifications to an existing spreadsheet.*
- *Save a new or existing spreadsheet.*
- *Use the application Help functions.*
- *Change the spreadsheet view mode.*
- *Use the page view magnification tool/zoom tool.*
- *Modify the toolbar display.*
- *Save an existing spreadsheet under another file format.*

1.1. First Steps with Spreadsheets

Before we begin we need to check whether Microsoft Excel is already installed on your PC. Click on the **Start** button and select the **Programs** option. You should see a list of installed programs, Excel may be listed here or it may be under the **Microsoft Office** option, this depends on how your system has been setup, as in the example in Figure 1.1.

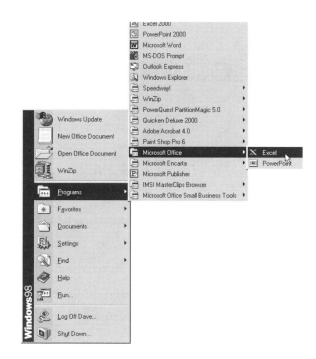

Figure 1.1 Starting Excel from the Start button.

Note that there may be other Microsoft Office programs also installed on your PC, such as Word, Access, or PowerPoint. However, it should be fairly obvious whether Excel is installed or not.

information

If Microsoft Excel is not already installed on your PC you should follow the instructions for setting up the software as detailed in the Office 97 "Getting Started" guide. These instructions are quite straightforward but if you have any difficulty installing the software then seek advice from your computer supplier or system administrator.

★ ECDL ★

Assuming that Excel is installed on your PC we are now ready to start learning how to use it to create and edit spreadsheets. Excel is an extremely flexible package and can be used to create a wide variety of different spreadsheets that can be used for different purposes. Your Excel spreadsheets can be as simple or as complicated as you like and you will soon learn how to create basic spreadsheets that can be enhanced to produce professional looking reports.

In this initial section we will look at some basic procedures which will allow us to:

● Open a spreadsheet application.
● Open an existing spreadsheet – make some modifications and save.
● Open several spreadsheets.
● Create a new spreadsheet and save.
● Save an existing spreadsheet onto the hard disk or a diskette.
● Close the spreadsheet.
● Use application Help functions.
● Close the spreadsheet application.

Exercise 1.1

In this exercise we will look at what happens when you start Excel and how to proceed to open, close and save spreadsheets (also referred to as Workbooks). We will also look at how you can access the Help facilities within Excel as and when you need them.

definition

Spreadsheet, Workbook, and Worksheets: Whilst Excel is recognised as a spreadsheet application Microsoft have adopted the terms Workbook and Worksheet to describe two different aspects of the package. The term Workbook refers to the actual spreadsheet file and a Workbook can consist of a number of separate Worksheets. In other words a Workbook is a collection of spreadsheets. Things will become clearer when we look at each of these elements in turn.

step **1.** Open Excel by selecting it from the **Start I Programs** option on the **Task Bar** as in the example in Figure 1.1 above.

Each time you start the Excel program you will see that a new blank Workbook is automatically opened at the same time and by default this Workbook contains 3 separate Worksheets shown as tabbed sections at the bottom of the screen, labelled **Sheet1**, **Sheet2**, and **Sheet3**, as in Figure 1.2.

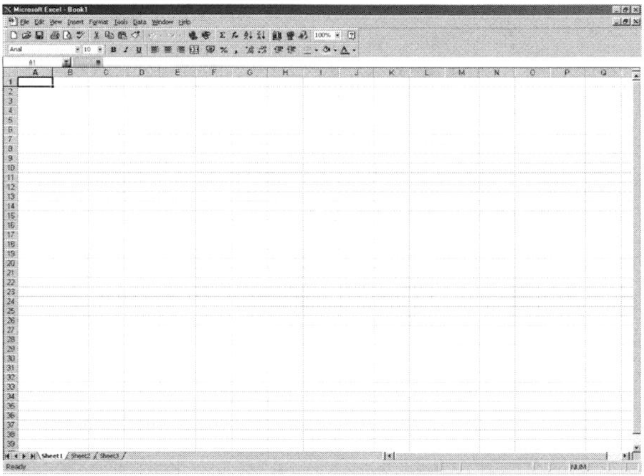

Figure 1.2 Excel opens a new blank spreadsheet when it is started.

Here you have the choice of using the blank Workbook to create your own spreadsheets from scratch or opening an existing Workbook.

2. For the moment we will ignore the creation of new spreadsheets and concentrate on opening an existing Workbook instead. To open an existing Workbook click on the **File I Open...** option on the Menu Bar at the top of the screen.

The **Open file** dialogue box should appear and by default the folder **My Documents** is displayed, as in Figure 1.3.

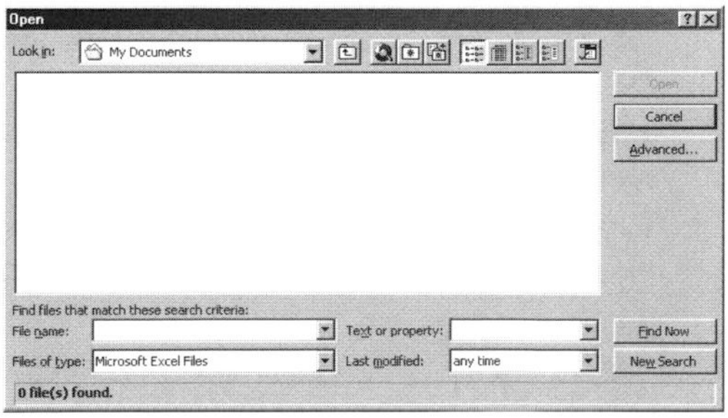

Figure 1.3 The Open File dialogue box showing the My Documents folder.

Don't be alarmed if there are no Workbooks displayed for you to open. The chances are that if this is the first time you have run Excel there will be no Workbooks in the **My Documents** folder so we will need to look somewhere else to find some existing Workbooks to open.

Using the **Look in:** drop down list, select **C:\Windows\Program Files\ Office97\Office** folder. Once selected you should see an entry called **Xl8galry.xls** and you should now select this and click on the **Open** button.

The **Xl8galry** Workbook should now be loaded and your screen should look as in Figure 1.4.

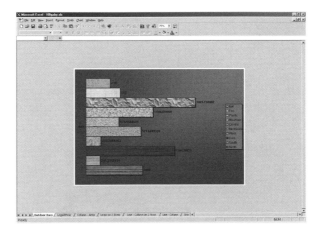

Figure 1.4 Excel main screen after opening the Xl8galry Workbook file.

The instructions above assume that when Microsoft Office was installed on your computer the standard default locations were used. If this is not the case then the file Xl8galry.xls may be located somewhere else and you will have to use the Find options in the Open file dialogue box to locate it. If the file does not exist on your hard disk you can open it from the Office folder on the Microsoft Office CD-Rom.

information

> Once Xl8galry.xls has been opened in Excel you may think
> that it doesn't look much like a spreadsheet and you would
> be right because this particular Workbook consists solely
> of charts or graphs, a feature of Excel which we will cover
> later. For the moment however, we will use this Workbook
> just to demonstrate some of the file management
> procedures available in Excel.

step **3.** Before we proceed any further we will make a copy of the Workbook
XL8galry.xls by saving a new version of it in the **My Documents** folder
via the following steps:

step **4.** On the **Menu Bar** click on **File | Save As...** and the **Save As** dialogue
box will appear, as in Figure 1.5.

**Figure 1.5 The Save As dialogue box with the file
name highlighted.**

step **5.** Select the **My Documents** folder using the **Save in:** drop down list and
type the filename *Excel1* in the **File name:** box, check that the **Save as
type:** box says **Microsoft Excel Workbook** and click on the **Save**
button.

You can Open several different Excel Workbooks at the same time by
following steps 1 and 2 above and selecting the appropriate folders from
which to load files. Similarly you can save any Excel Workbooks by following
steps 4 and 5 changing both the folder and filenames as appropriate.

step **6.** To close a Workbook click on the **File | Close** option on the **Menu Bar**.

★ ECDL ★

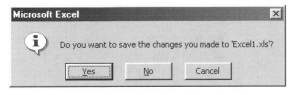

caution!

If you have made any changes to an open Workbook, then when you try to close it you will be asked whether you wish to save the changes you have made to the file, for example as in Figure 1.6

Microsoft Excel	✕

Do you want to save the changes you made to 'Excel1.xls'?

Yes   No   Cancel

Figure 1.6 The warning displayed if you attempt to close an unsaved Workbook.

If you click on the **Yes** button then the file will be saved with the existing filename – overwriting the original version. However, if you wish to keep the original version of the file you should click on the **No** button and use the **File I Save As...** option from the **Menu Bar** to save the current open Workbook with a different filename from the original.

Finally in this exercise we will look at the Help facilities available in Excel which can provide you with online assistance when you need it. There are several different ways to trigger the Help functions within Excel and we will deal with each method in turn.

7. When you started Excel you may have noticed a small window as shown in step Figure 1.7. (If this window doesn't appear simply press the F1 key on your keyboard.)

Figure 1.7 The Office Assistant.

This is the Office Assistant and it is designed to provide you with help if you encounter problems when using the Excel program. The Office Assistant like the normal Microsoft Help facilities is context sensitive which means that it tries to provide help based on what you are doing at the time.

information

There are several different "characters" available to act as Office Assistants and depending on how your version of Microsoft Office has been configured you may see any of the following characters shown in Figure 1.8.

Figure 1.8 The various Office Assistant "characters".

If you click on the **Office Assistant** then the following pop up dialogue box appears, as in Figure 1.9.

Figure 1.9 The Office Assistant asks you what you would like to do.

As you can see from the example in Figure 1.9 one of the best features of the Office Assistant is that you can simply type in a question and it will try to find the most appropriate help for you.

For example, type in the words *Saving my work* and click on the **Search** button. The Office Assistant should display a list of topics similar to that in Figure 1.10 for you to choose from.

Figure 1.10 Performing a query using the Office Assistant.

Clicking on an item in the list will display the relevant Help topic.

8. As well as the Office Assistant you can access Help by clicking on the **Help |
Contents and Index** option on the **Menu Bar**. This displays a window
with 3 tabbed sections: **Contents**, **Index** and **Find**.

**Figure 1.11 The Help Topics Contents tab showing
sub sections.**

The **Contents** tab presents you with a list of Help contents for you to select
from. Note that the main sections may have sub-sections, as in Figure 1.11.

Figure 1.12 You can search for keywords in the Index section.

The **Index** tab displays a list of indexed keywords that are available in the help system. You simply click on the index word you want and then click on the **Display** button as in Figure 1.12.

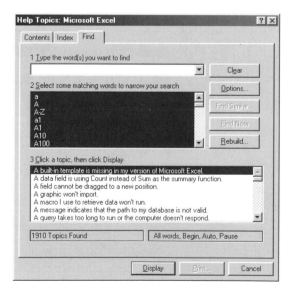

Figure 1.13 The Find sections let you look for words or phrases.

The **Find** tab allows you to search for any word or phrase and the Help system will then show you any matches that it can find. Once again you can simply click on any found topic and click on the **Display** button to see it, as in Figure 1.13.

shortcut

> **Help is always available in Excel no matter what task you are performing. The quickest way to get help is to press the F1 on your keyboard.**

Whichever method you use to access the Help system in Excel you will be able to see step by step help on most topics as in Figure 1.14.

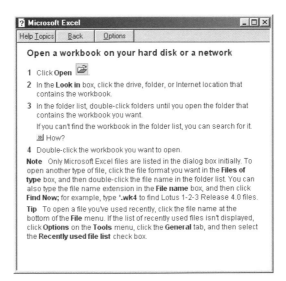

Figure 1.14 A specific Help Topic on how to Open a Workbook.

Summary

In this initial section on Excel we have covered the procedures necessary to start the application and to open any existing Workbook files. We have also looked at how to save Workbooks and how to use both the Office Assistant and the Help system to obtain help relevant to the procedures being carried out.

Fortunately, these basic tasks are common to all the modules in Microsoft Office, so once you have mastered these procedures in Excel you should be able to cope with the same tasks in the other applications, such as Word or PowerPoint.

1.2. Adjust Basic Settings

Now that we have looked at starting Excel and opening and saving Workbooks we need to investigate the main Excel screen in more detail.

In this section we will learn how to:

● Change the spreadsheet view mode.
● Use the page view magnification tool/zoom tool.
● Modify the toolbar display.

Exercise 1.2

In this exercise we will look at how you can alter the way that Excel displays information and how you can alter the appearance of Excel itself.

If it is not already open you should start Excel and, if for some reason a blank Workbook isn't displayed simply click on **File | New...** on the **Menu Bar** and a tabbed dialogue box as shown in Figure 1.15 should be displayed.

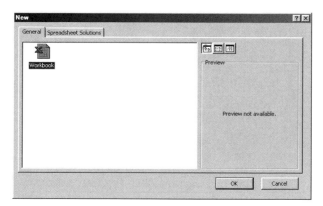

Figure 1.15 Creating a new blank Excel Workbook.

Click on the **OK** button to create a new blank Workbook and your display should now look like the example in Figure 1.16. If the **Office Assistant** window is displayed then close it by clicking on the **Close** button in the top right hand corner.

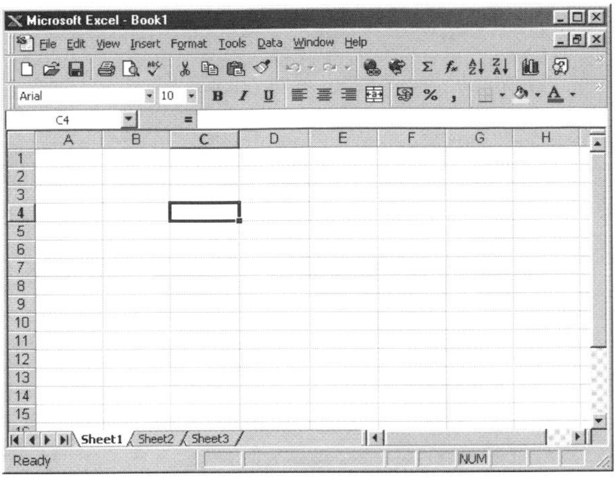

Figure 1.16 A blank new Workbook with a cell selected.

The example in Figure 1.16 shows the Normal view of an open Workbook but there are some options available for changing the display.

1. First of all click on cell reference **E9** with the mouse and type the word *Test* followed by the Return or Enter key on your keyboard.

2. Next, select **View I Page Break Preview** on the **Menu Bar** and you should see the dialogue box shown in Figure 1.17. Just click on the **OK** button and it should disappear. Now you will see something like the example in Figure 1.18. This is the **Page Break Preview** view which shows us where the word **Test** would be printed on a piece of paper. Select **View I Normal** to return to the standard view of the Workbook.

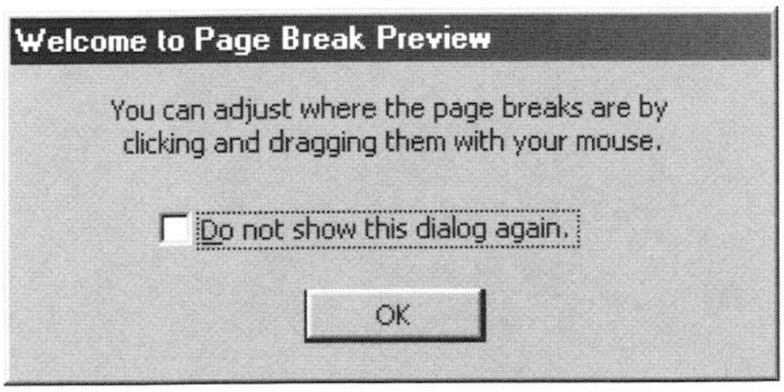

Figure 1.17 Welcome to Page Break Preview.

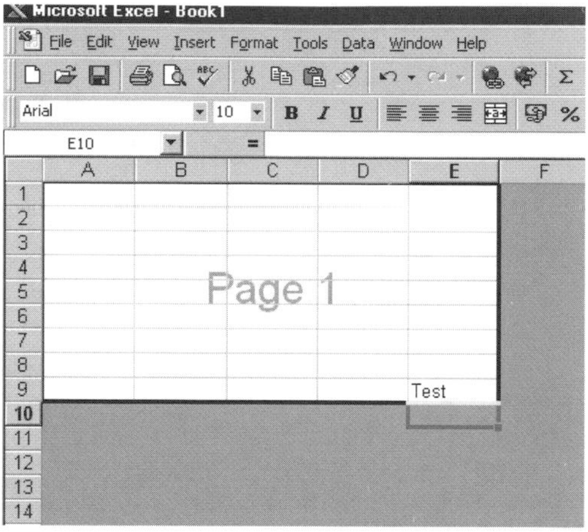

Figure 1.18 The Page Break Preview view.

step **3.** Also on the **View** menu we can select **Full Screen view** which just displays the **Menu Bar** and the Workbook itself without any toolbars or the status bar visible, as in Figure 1.19. To return to the **Normal** view click on the **Close Full Screen** button.

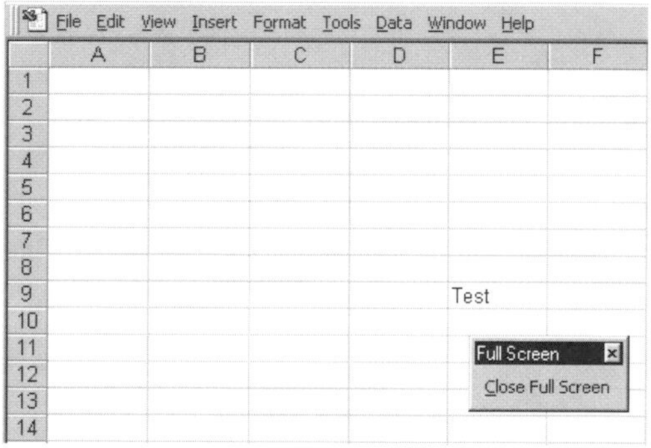

Figure 1.19 The Full Screen view with the Close Full Screen button.

As well as switching views as just described, Excel offers a Zoom feature which basically allows us to magnify the current Worksheet being displayed.

Controlling the magnification or zoom level can be achieved in two ways:

step **4.** By using the **Zoom** icon control drop down list on the **Standard** Toolbar, as in Figure 1.20.

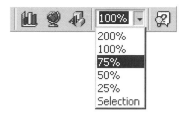

Figure 1.20 Using the Zoom icon to change magnification.

5. Or, by using the **View I Zoom...** option from the **Menu Bar**, which displays a window as in Figure 1.21. Here you can select several preset levels of magnification or type in your own preference in the **Custom:** box.

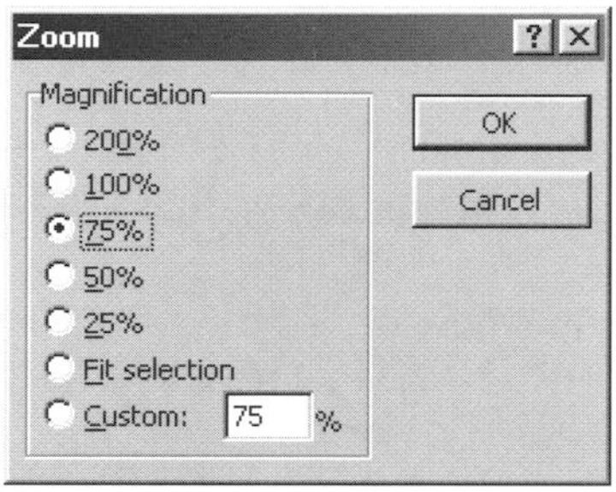

Figure 1.21 The Zoom control window.

6. Whichever method you use to adjust the Zoom level the area of the screen displaying the Worksheet will magnify or shrink the image relative to the main Excel window, as in Figure 1.22.

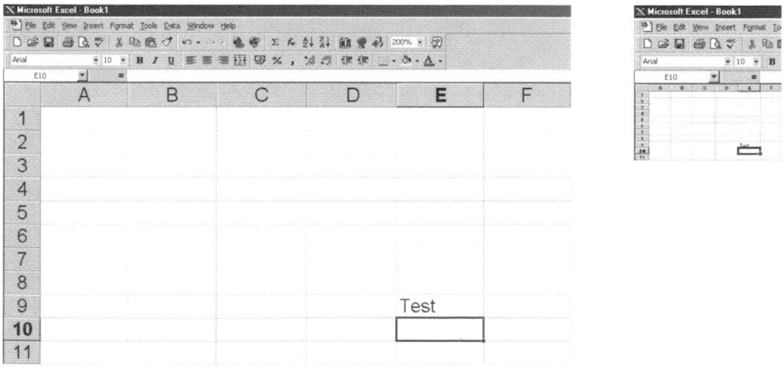

Figure 1.22 Different Zoom levels, 200% on the left and 50% on the right.

Notice that the **Menu Bar** and the toolbars are the same size but the spreadsheet area is a different size.

Finally in this exercise we shall look at how you modify the Toolbar displayed in Excel.

Excel has a total of 13 separate toolbars available. However, by default only 2 of these are displayed at the top of the screen. The topmost is normally the **Standard** Toolbar (Figure 1.23) and just below it is the **Formatting** Toolbar (Figure 1.24).

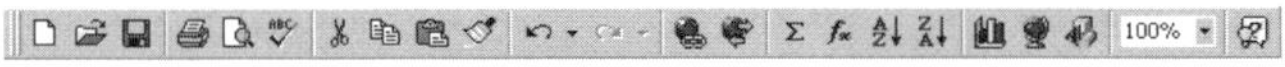

Figure 1.23 The Standard Toolbar (top of screen by default)

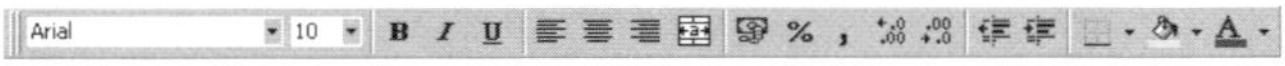

Figure 1.24 The Formatting Toolbar (top of screen by default)

7. You can control which of the 13 toolbars are visible by using the **View I Toolbars** option on the **Menu Bar**. Toolbars currently displayed are shown with a tick next to them as in Figure 1.25.

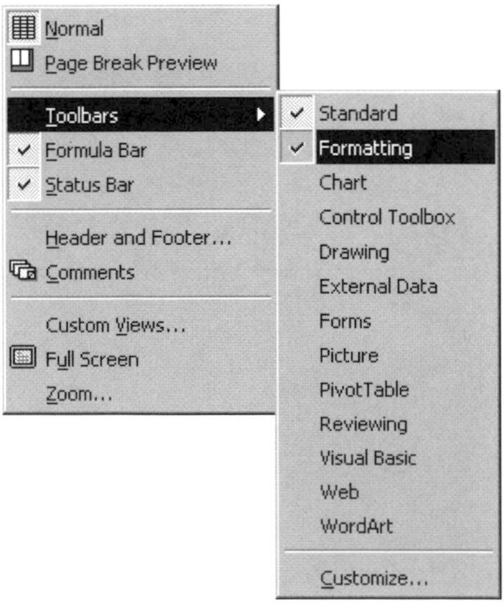

Figure 1.25 Selecting toolbars for displaying.

Finally, close the Workbook by clicking on **File | Close** on the **Menu Bar**. Despite the fact that this spreadsheet only has a single entry in one cell we will use it in the next exercise, so, when you are asked whether you want to save the changes you made to **Book1.xls** you should click on **Yes** and save the Workbook in the **My Documents** folder with the name *Test*.

Summary

In this section on Excel we have looked at how you can display Worksheets in various ways such as the Normal view, the Page Break Preview view, and the Full Screen view. We have also looked at how you can use the Zoom controls to increase or decrease the size of the Worksheet image being viewed. In addition, we looked at how to control the displaying of Toolbars in Excel.

You should now have a better understanding of the main elements of the Excel screen and how to control and manage the display of information.

1.3. Document Exchange

Excel uses its own file format with the file extension .xls for storing Workbooks. However, there may be occasions when you need to save a spreadsheet in a different format, for example, to transfer text into a word processing package or to use spreadsheet data in a database.

In this section we will look at how you can:

● Save an existing spreadsheet under another file format: txt file, document template, software type or version number etc.
● Save a document in a format appropriate for posting to a Web Site.

Exercise 1.3

This exercise will look at how you can save Excel spreadsheets or parts thereof in different formats.

If it is not already open you should start Excel and open the **Test.xls** Workbook which we saved in the **My Documents** folder in Exercise 1.1.

step **1.** When you click on the **File | Save As...** option on the **Menu Bar** the **Save As...** dialogue box appears, as in Figure 1.26.

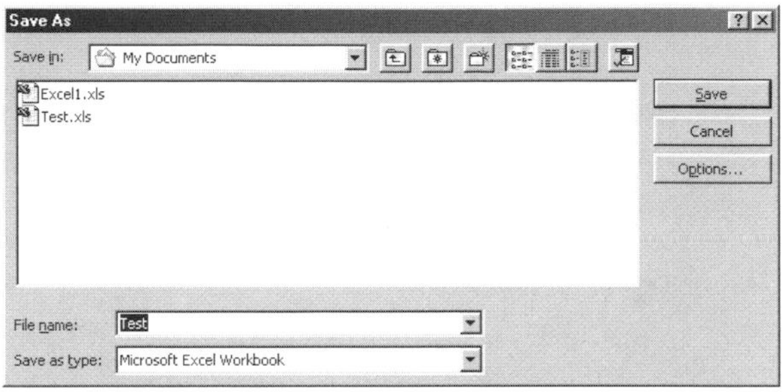

Figure 1.26 The Save As... dialogue box where you can decide on the target folder and file name.

2. As well as being able to specify a filename and a location (folder) for saving the Workbook you can also specify the file type by clicking on the drop down list on the **Save as type:** box as in Figure 1.27.

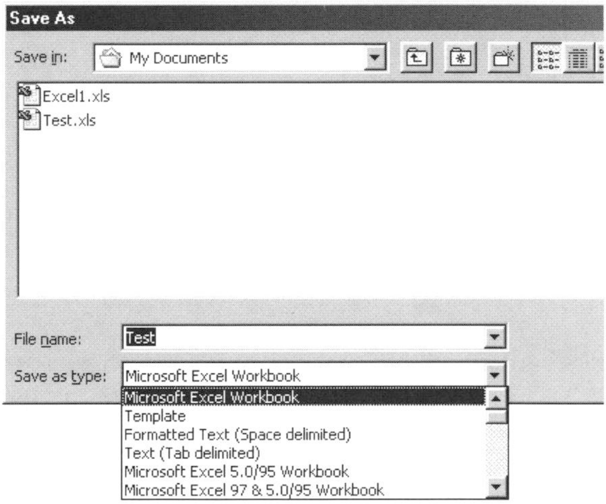

Figure 1.27 Using the Save as type option to save a Worksheet in a different file format.

Excel allows you to save a spreadsheet in the following file formats:

Save as type	Extension	Use to save
Excel 97 & 5.0/95 Workbook	.xls	A normal Excel spreadsheet.
Excel 97 Template	.xlt	A Workbook as a template for creating similar spreadsheets.
Excel version 5.0/95 Workbook	.xls	A spreadsheet for use with a previous version of Excel.

Excel version 4.0 Workbook	.xls	A spreadsheet for use with a previous version of Excel.
Excel version 4.0 Worksheet	.xls	A spreadsheet for use with a previous version of Excel.
Excel 3.0 Worksheet	.xls	A spreadsheet for use with a previous version of Excel.
Excel 2.x Worksheet	.xls	A spreadsheet for use with a previous version of Excel.
Lotus 1-2-3 Release 4	.wk4	An Excel spreadsheet suitable format for use with a specific version of Lotus 1-2-3.
Lotus 1-2-3 Release 3	.wk3	An Excel spreadsheet suitable format for use with a specific version of Lotus 1-2-3.
Lotus 1-2-3 Release 2.x	.wk1	An Excel spreadsheet suitable format for use with a specific version of Lotus 1-2-3.
Lotus 1-2-3 Release 1.x	.wks	An Excel spreadsheet suitable format for use with a specific version of Lotus 1-2-3.
Quattro Pro for MS-DOS	.wq1	An Excel spreadsheet suitable format for use with Quattro Pro.
dBASE	.dbf	Spreadsheet data in a specific database format.
CSV (Comma delimited)	.csv	Spreadsheet data in a general database format.
Text (Tab delimited)	.txt	Spreadsheet data for use in a word processing application.

In addition, you can save the data in an Excel Workbook in a format that is suitable for creating Web pages on the Internet. However, you cannot do this with the normal **File | Save As...** option on the **Menu Bar** and instead you have to use another menu option.

3. Clicking on the **File | Save as HTML...** option on the **Menu Bar** starts the **Save as HTML Wizard** which displays the dialogue box shown in Figure 1.28.

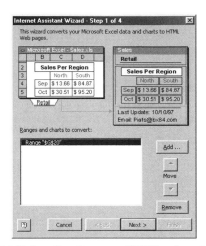

Figure 1.28 Using the Save as HTML wizard to save a Worksheet as a Web page.

From here all you need to do is click on the **Next** button and then follow the instructions to save your Excel Workbook data in a format suitable for publishing Web pages on the Internet.

Wizard: A Wizard within Microsoft applications is a special feature which is designed to guide the user step by step through a complex process. There are many different types of Wizards included as standard with Microsoft Office. In addition if you have access to the Internet you can download other Wizards that you might find useful from:

http://www.microsoft.com/downloads/search.asp?

Summary

In this section we have covered the ways that you can save Excel spreadsheets in various formats so that the information they contain can be used in other applications such as Microsoft Word or other spreadsheet packages like Lotus 1-2-3. We have also seen how it is possible to generate Web pages so that Excel spreadsheet data can be used on the Internet.

Review Questions

1. What is the basic procedure for starting Excel from the Windows desktop?

2. What is the difference between a Worksheet and a Workbook?

3. When you start a new Workbook how many blank Worksheets are provided as standard?

4. Which keyboard key should you press to invoke the online Help in Excel?

5. Which 2 toolbars are displayed onscreen by default in Excel?

6. Which Menu Bar option would you use to save a spreadsheet in a format suitable for publishing as a Web page?

7. What is a Wizard?

2

Basic Operations

In this chapter you will learn how to

- *Enter numbers, text and simple Formulas into a cell.*
- *Use the undo command.*
- *Select cells, rows and columns.*
- *Use the Copy and Paste tools to duplicate and move cell contents.*
- *Move or Copy cell contents between active Worksheets and Workbooks.*
- *Delete cell contents in a selected cell range.*
- *Search and replace specified cell content.*
- *Insert and delete rows and columns.*
- *Modify column width and row height.*
- *Sort selected data in alphabetic or numerical order.*

★ ECDL ★

Now that we have overcome the initial hurdle of Getting Started and covered the First Steps with Spreadsheets it is time to look at the Basic Operations that can be performed with Excel.

However, before we delve into the package too deeply we need to understand a few preliminary concepts regarding navigating our way around spreadsheets.

As described in the introduction to this guide, spreadsheets consist of a vast number of cells arranged in the form of a grid. In Excel each cell is referenced by a set of co-ordinates based on its column and row position, for example, A1, D12, AD1020, etc. Each Worksheet has a total of 256 columns referenced as A through IV and 65536 rows number consecutively 1 through 65536. This means that a single Excel Worksheet has a total of 16,777,216 individual cells for us to use.

By default in Excel, gridlines are used to display the individual cells on a Worksheet and the currently active cell is evident by means of a dark border, as in Figure 2.1.

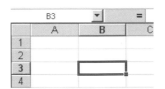

Figure 2.1 The current active cell marker.

You can move the active cell marker in two ways. Using the cursor control keys on the keyboard up, down, left or right and by clicking on any inactive cell with the mouse. Note that the mouse pointer is displayed as a ✛ when moved across the grid of cells. As you change from one active cell to another the cell reference is automatically updated. Try out these two different methods so that you become familiar with both. Understanding how to navigate around a spreadsheet is a basic skill which is essential for the next step of this guide.

2.1. Insert Data

We have now reached the point were we can start to insert data into a Worksheet and begin to see how Excel can be used for a variety of different tasks.

In this section you will learn how to:

● Enter numbers in a cell.
● Enter text in a cell.
● Enter symbols or special characters in a cell.
● Enter simple Formulas in a cell.
● Use the undo command.

Exercise 2.1

This exercise will involve creating a new Workbook and looking at the options available for entering various types of data and Formulae into spreadsheet cells. We will also see how it is possible to correct any mistakes that we make by taking advantage of Excel's 'Undo' Function.

step **1.** If it is not already running start Excel and create a new Workbook by selecting **File | New...** from the **Menu Bar**. Your screen should now look like the example in Figure 2.2.

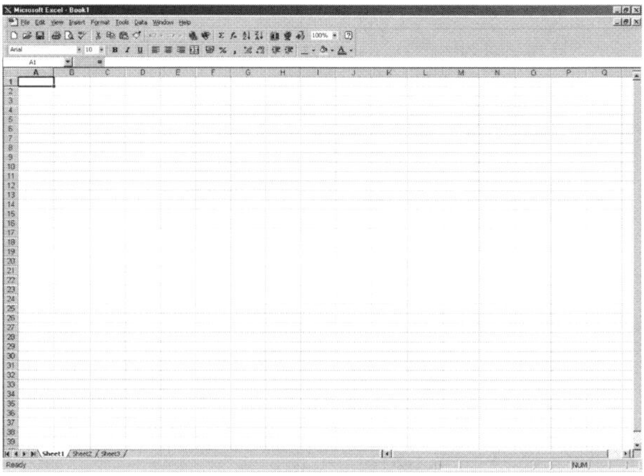

Figure 2.2 Excel with a new Workbook opened.

step **2.** Next, with the active cell marker at position **A1** type the digits *34* and press the Return or Enter key on your keyboard. The active cell marker should automatically move down to cell **A2**. (If **A2** is not the active cell use the cursor keys or the mouse to make it active.) Now following the same procedure enter the following numbers in these specific cells:

Cell Reference	Value
A2	11
A3	25
A4	9

Your Worksheet should now look like the example in Figure 2.3. Notice how the numbers which we have entered have been aligned on the right hand side of the cells, this is the default action in Excel when you enter numeric values.

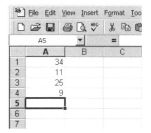

Figure 2.3 Entering numeric data into a Worksheet.

3. Now move the active cell marker to position **B1** either by using the cursor keys on the keyboard or by clicking on cell **B1** with the mouse. Once cell **B1** is active, type the word *Apples* and press the Return or Enter key on your keyboard. Again the active cell marker should automatically move downwards so that cell **B2** becomes active. Following the same procedure enter the following text in these specific cells:

Cell Reference	Text
B2	*Oranges*
B3	*Bananas*
B4	*Melons*

Your Worksheet should now look like the example in Figure 2.4. Notice how the text has been aligned towards the left hand side of the cells, this is the default action in Excel when you enter text.

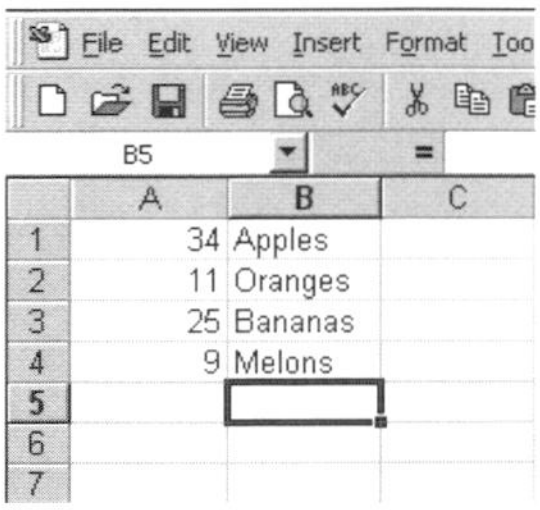

Figure 2.4 Entering text into a Worksheet.

Occasionally you might need to enter a symbol or special character in a cell, for example the ¥ (Yen) currency character or a symbol such as a © (copyright). Normally these characters are not readily available directly from the keyboard unless a specific font such as Symbol or Wingdings is being used. Fortunately there are two ways in which you can insert special characters into a cell. Method one – if you know the right code (refer to an ASCII table) you can hold down the Alt key on your keyboard and simply type in the relevant numbers, then when you release the Alt key the character or symbol will appear. For example, Alt and 0165 produces the ¥ symbol and Alt 0169 generates the © symbol. Method two – start the standard Windows Character Map application by selecting Programs I Accessories I System Tools I Character Map from the Start button on the Taskbar. Using this program you can select any of the characters or symbols displayed to be inserted into your spreadsheet cell. The advantage of the second method is that you can actually see the characters that you wish to select and if necessary change to a different font such as Wingdings to find a particular character or symbol.

4. As well as entering numbers and text in cells we can also enter Formulas which can be used to perform calculations. Let's start by entering a simple Formula in cell **A5** to add up all the Apples and Oranges. Make sure that cell **A5** is the active cell and type in the following Formula: $=a1+a2$

5. When you press the Return or Enter key Excel automatically performs the calculation and displays the result in the cell containing the Formula. Your Worksheet should now look like the example in Figure 2.5.

Figure 2.5 Entering a simple Formula into a cell.

6. If you now move the active cell marker back to cell **A5** you will see that the Formula used to add the number of Apples and Oranges is displayed in the **Formula Bar** as in Figure 2.6.

A5	▼	=	=A1+A2	
	A	**B**	**C**	**D**
1	34	Apples		
2	11	Oranges		
3	25	Bananas		
4	9	Melons		
5	45			
6				
7				

Figure 2.6 The Formula used in A5 is displayed in the Formula Bar.

7. Excel provides hundreds of Formulas which can be used to make lots of different types of calculations. Let's try out another type of calculation by typing in the following, also into cell **A5** thereby overwriting the existing simple addition of two numbers:

=sum(a1:a4)

Once again when you press Return or Enter the result of the calculation appears in cell **A5** as in the example shown in Figure 2.7.

A5	▼	=	=SUM(A1:A4)	
	A	**B**	**C**	**D**
1	34	Apples		
2	11	Oranges		
3	25	Bananas		
4	9	Melons		
5	79			
6				
7				

Figure 2.7 Using the Sum Formula to total a series of numbers.

In this instance the Formula tells Excel to add up all the numbers in cells **A1**, **A2**, **A3**, and **A4** to produce a total of all the fruit. We could have achieved the same result using the Formula =A1+A2+A3+A4 but Excel allows us to specify a range of contiguous cells by using the colon character (:) between the cell references in the Formula. This is very useful when you wish to perform a calculation on a long list of numbers. Before we move on to the next step type the word *Total* in cell **B5** just to remind us to what the figure in **A5** refers.

shortcut

> **Excel has a very useful feature known as AutoSum which is available on the Standard Toolbar. If you click once on this icon then Excel will highlight a range of cells adjacent to the active cell as a 'best guess' to what requires summing, as in Figure 2.8. If you wish to accept the selected range then you simply press the Return or Enter key and Excel will automatically place the correct Formula in the active cell for you.**

SUM	▼	✗ ✓	=	=SUM(A1:A4)
	A	B	C	D
1	34	Apples		
2	11	Oranges		
3	25	Bananas		
4	9	Melons		
5	=SUM(A1:A4)			
6				
7				

Figure 2.8 Using the AutoSum feature.

8. By default all Formulas in Excel Worksheets are recalculated automatically. This means that if we alter any of the numbers referenced by a Formula the result will change accordingly. For example, move the active cell marker to cell **A2** and type the number *12* to replace the **11** that is already there. This time when you press the Return or Enter key, the total figure (**79**) automatically changes to **80** as shown in Figure 2.9.

A3	▼		=	25
	A	B	C	
1	34	Apples		
2	12	Oranges		
3	25	Bananas		
4	9	Melons		
5	80	Total		
6				
7				

Figure 2.9 Automatic recalculation of the Total in action.

This is probably the most important feature of a spreadsheet application such as Excel. The ability to perform calculations automatically and to recalculate the results when the underlying data changes, make spreadsheets a practically essential tool for many users, especially in the business world.

9. Excel has a special feature called 'Undo' which can be extremely useful if we make a mistake when entering data. Using our current example Worksheet if you select the **Edit | Undo** option from the **Menu Bar** then the contents of cell **A2** will revert back to the original value of **11** (as it was before we

★ ECDL ★

replaced it with the number **12**). Notice also that the **Total** is recalculated to reflect the change as well, as in Figure 2.10.

caution!

The actual wording of the Edit I Undo option on the Menu Bar depends on whatever the last operation carried out by Excel was. As a result the word Undo could be followed by other words which describe what the last action was and what will be undone when you execute the command.

| A2 | ▼ | = | 11 |

	A	B	C
1	34	Apples	
2	11	Oranges	
3	25	Bananas	
4	9	Melons	
5	79	Total	
6			

Figure 2.10 The example Worksheet after performing an Undo command.

shortcut

You can access the Undo feature quickly by clicking once on the Undo icon on the Standard Toolbar. Each time you click on it the last action in undone, therefore you can undo several mistakes or previous changes if necessary.

10. step Finally in this section you should save the current Workbook in the **My Documents** folder using the file name *Fruit*.

information

When you enter digits into a cell Excel recognises them as numbers and conversely when you enter letters Excel interprets them as text. Mixing digits with letters always results in Excel interpreting the entry as text. However, on occasion you may need to enter digits or numbers so that they are treated solely as text. To do this simply place a single quote character at the beginning of the numbers you wish to enter, like this '1999 or '2000 and they will appear as text in the cell.

Summary

In this section we have seen how both numbers and text can be entered into Worksheet cells. Remember that by default, numbers are aligned to the right and text aligned to the left within cells. We have also seen that Formulas can be placed in cells to perform various types of calculation and if the referenced data changes then the Formula automatically recalculates the result.

In addition, we have learned that the Undo feature of Excel allows us to step backwards and reverse any actions which we have previously carried out.

2.2. Select Data

Now that we have a simple spreadsheet of our own to work with we can start looking at the various ways that we can select areas of a Worksheet in order to perform actions on complete ranges of cells. In this section you will learn how to do the following:

● Select a cell or range of adjacent or non-adjacent cells.
● Select a row or column.
● Select a range of adjacent or non-adjacent rows or columns.

Exercise 2.2

1. If it is not already running start Excel and Open the Workbook called **Fruit** which we saved earlier in the **My Documents** folder. Your screen should now look like the example in Figure 2.11.

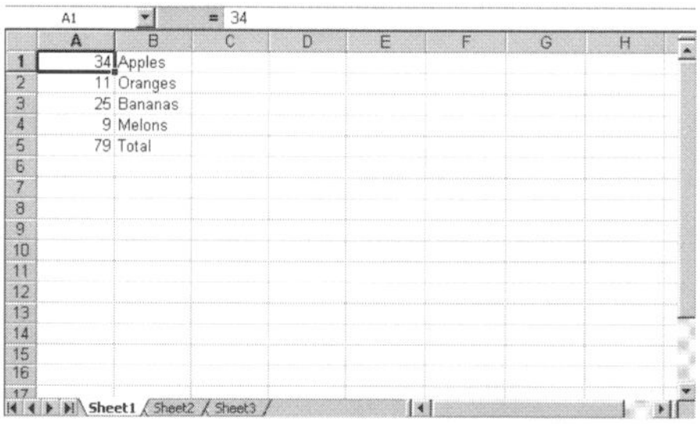

Figure 2.11 The Fruit Workbook after opening.

2. To select multiple cells simply click on any cell and whilst holding hold the left mouse button drag the ✥ pointer across the grid of cells and they will turn black as they are selected. Release the mouse button when your selection is complete. On the **Fruit** Worksheet use this method to select all the cells in the range **D6** to **G14** and your display should look like Figure 2.12.

★ ★ ★
★ ★
★ ECDL ★
★ ★
★ ★ ★

information

When selecting cells with the mouse, if you drag the pointer to any of the window boundaries then Excel will simply scroll the Worksheet automatically to allow you to extend the selection beyond the area normally visible.

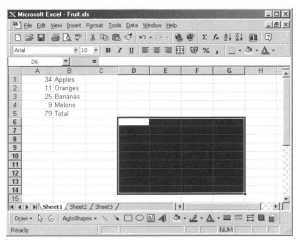

Figure 2.12 Cells D6 to G14 selected.

To deselect a selected range of cells simply click once with the left mouse button on any non-selected cell and the selection will disappear.

shortcut

An alternative method of selecting a range of cells is by using the keyboard. If you hold down the Shift key and use the cursor control keys you can extend the range of selected cells outwards from the current active cell.

3. Normally cell range selection is done on adjacent cells but if you need to select non-adjacent cells you can do this simply by holding down the Ctrl key on the keyboard and then clicking on the desired cells with the pointer, as shown in Figure 2.13.

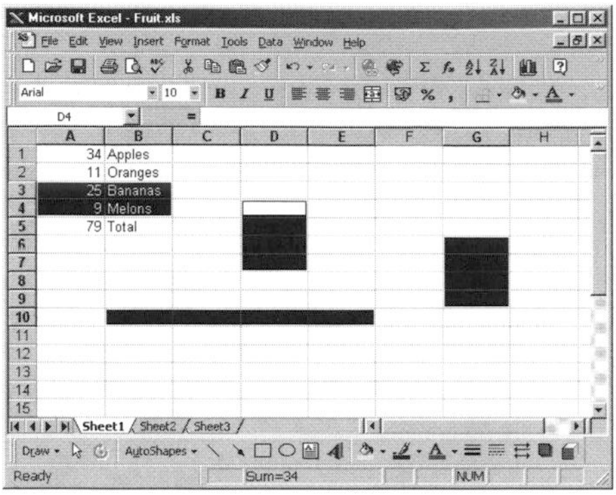

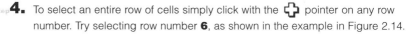

Figure 2.13 Selecting non-adjacent cells.

Once again clicking on any non selected cells after releasing the Ctrl key will deselect everything.

step**4.** To select an entire row of cells simply click with the ✛ pointer on any row number. Try selecting row number **6**, as shown in the example in Figure 2.14.

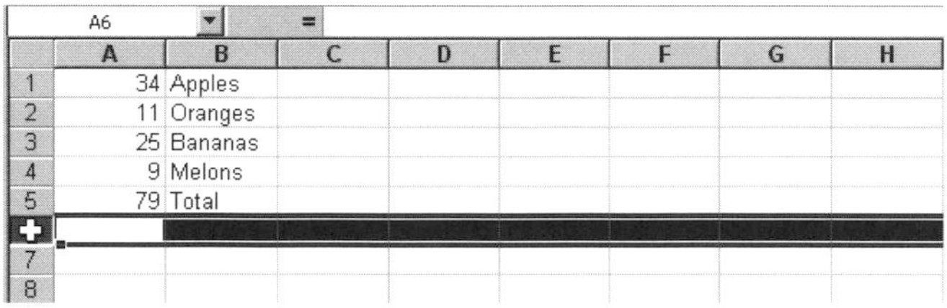

Figure 2.14 Selecting entire rows.

step**5.** Likewise if you need to select a complete column of cells just click with the pointer on any column letter. Try selecting column **D** in our **Fruit** Worksheet as the example in Figure 2.15 shows.

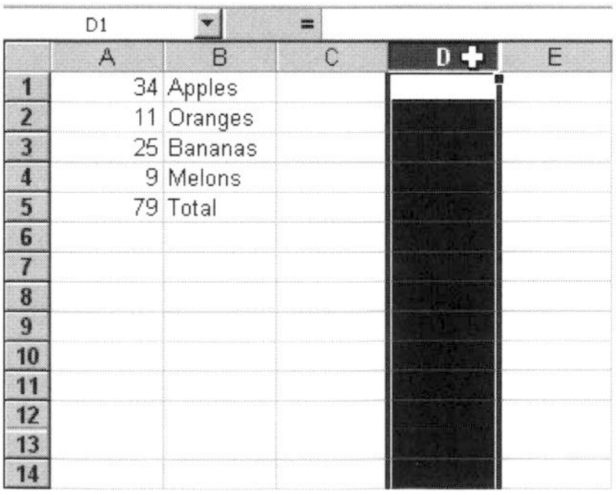

Figure 2.15 Selecting an entire column of cells.

★ ECDL ★

Just as when selecting adjacent cells, you can drag the pointer across multiple rows of numbers or column letters in order to select complete adjacent rows or columns.

6. Now suppose you need to select multiple non-adjacent rows or columns, well you can do this as well by holding down the Ctrl key whilst clicking with the pointer on the rows or columns you want to select, as shown in Figure 2.16. You can even select non adjacent rows and columns at the same time as in the example in Figure 2.17.

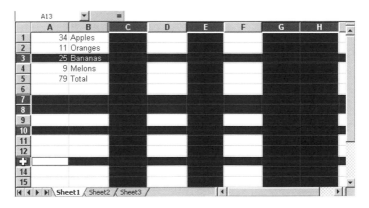

Figure 2.16 Non-adjacent rows selected.

Figure 2.17 Multiple rows and columns both adjacent and non-adjacent selected.

7. Finally on the subject of selecting cells there is a very quick and easy way to select the entire Worksheet. Simply click once with the pointer on the small grey box called the **Select All** button at the junction of the row numbers and column letters as shown in Figure 2.18 and all the cells will be selected.

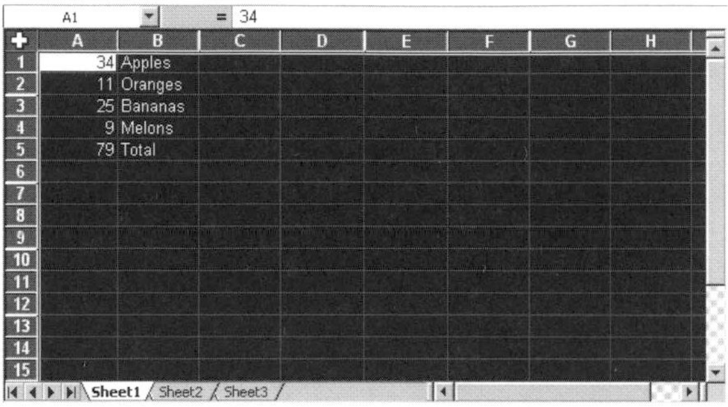

Figure 2.18 Selecting the entire Worksheet.

Summary

As we have seen, selecting cells is an important factor when using Excel and there are several different ways that this can be achieved. Adjacent ranges of cells can be selected as can adjacent rows or columns. Remember that to select non-adjacent cells, rows or columns you must hold down the Ctrl key whilst performing the selection process. Lastly we saw how to quickly select the entire Worksheet by just clicking on the Select All button.

2.3. Copy, Move, Delete

Now that we have seen how to select cell, rows, and columns we can put these procedures into some practical use by looking at copying, moving and deleting the contents of specific areas in our Worksheet.

In this section we will see how to:

- Use the Copy and Paste tools to duplicate cell contents in another part of a Worksheet.
- Use the Cut and Paste tools to move cell contents within a Worksheet.
- Move or Copy cell contents between active Worksheets.
- Move or Copy cell contents between active Workbooks.
- Delete cell contents in a selected cell range.

Exercise 2.3

step **1.** If it is not already running start Excel and Open the Workbook called **Fruit** which we saved earlier in the **My Documents** folder. Your screen should now look like the example in Figure 2.19.

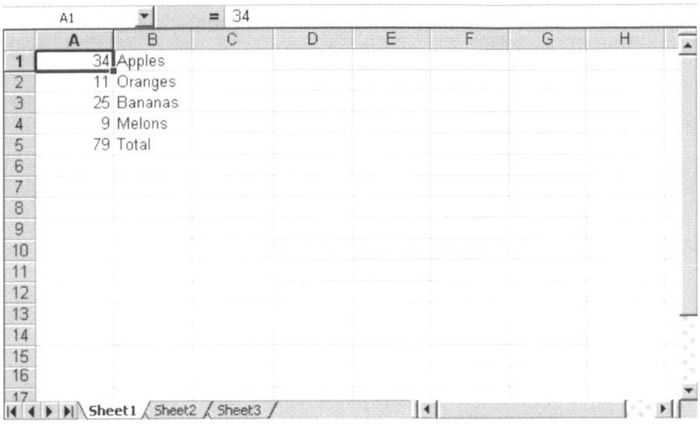

Figure 2.19 The Fruit Worksheet.

2. Using the ⊕ pointer select the cells in the range **B1:B5** and your Worksheet should now look like Figure 2.20.

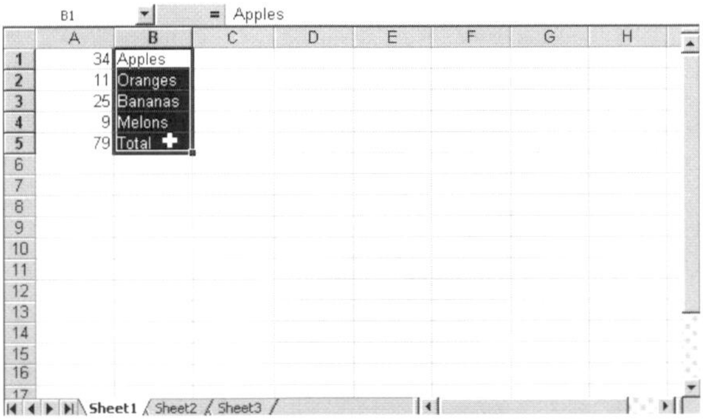

Figure 2.20 Selecting a cell range to copy.

3. Next, click on **Edit I Copy** on the **Menu Bar**. This makes a copy of the selected cells in the Windows Clipboard. Now, click once on cell **C7** to make it active and select **Edit I Paste** from the **Menu Bar**. An exact copy of the cell range **B1:B5** should now appear in the cell range **C7:C11** as the example in Figure 2.21 shows.

shortcut

You may have noticed the dotted, flashing outline that appear around the range B1:B5 when we copied it to the Clipboard. This is called the 'Marquee' and it is used to indicate which cells have been copied. To remove the Marquee press the Esc key on your keyboard.

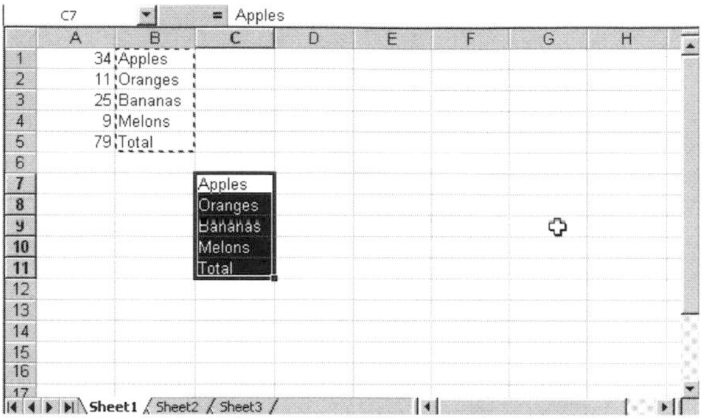

Figure 2.21 Pasting copied cells in a new location.

4. Next, select the cell range **A1:A5** and click on **Edit I Cut** on the **Menu Bar**. You will notice that the data in the range disappears as it has been removed from its original location and placed in the Clipboard. Make cell **D7** active and click on **Edit I Paste** on the **Menu Bar**. The contents of cell range **A1:A5** should now appear in the range **D7:D11** as shown in Figure 2.22.

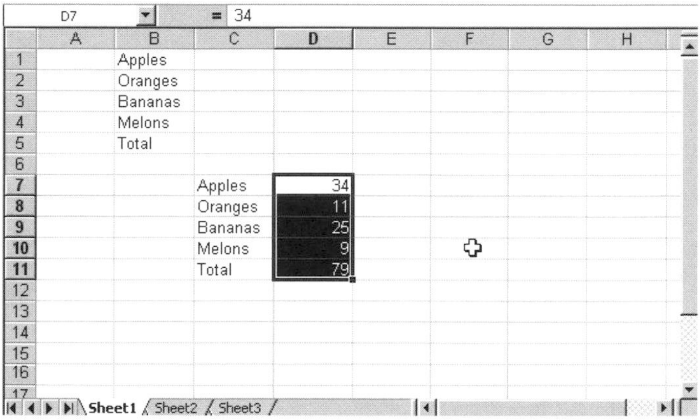

Figure 2.22 Moving a cell range using Cut and Paste.

shortcut

Instead of using the Menu Bar to perform Copy, Cut and Paste Functions via the Clipboard you can click on the appropriate icons on the Standard Toolbar.

5. As well as using the Copy, Cut and Paste Function either to copy or move a cell range within an active Worksheet they can be used to copy or move items to other Worksheets and even other Workbooks. For example, select the

range **C7:D11** and **Copy** it to the Clipboard. Next, click once on the tab labelled **Sheet2** which is near the bottom of the screen. This displays Worksheet number 2 in our Workbook which should be blank. Make cell **A1** active and now if you select **Edit | Paste** from the **Menu Bar** the contents of cell range **C7:D11** on **Sheet1** will be pasted into the cell range **A1:B5** as shown in Figure 2.23. Switch back to **Sheet1** by clicking on the appropriate tab and you will notice that its contents are still intact.

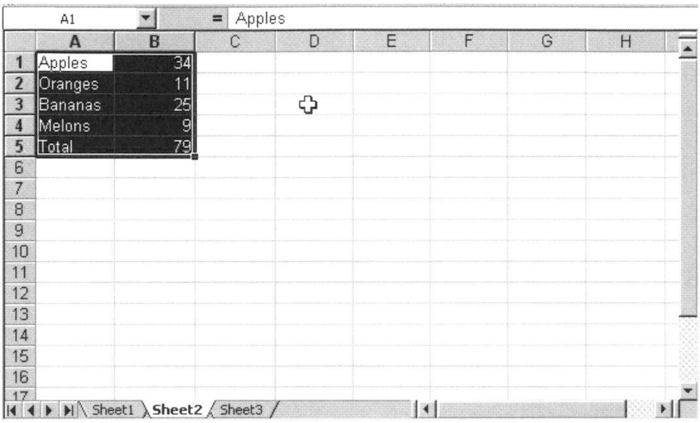

Figure 2.23 Sheet 2 after copying a range of cells from Sheet1.

6. To copy or move a cell range to another Workbook we can use the same procedure as described in step 5 above but instead of switching to **Sheet2** after copying or cutting to the Clipboard we need to switch to a different Workbook. For example, copy the cells **C7:D11** on our **Fruit** Workbook **Sheet1**, click on **File | New** on the **Menu Bar** and then click on **OK** to create a new Workbook. Now select **Edit | Paste** on the **Menu Bar** and the copied range of cells will appear in range **A1:B5** in our new Workbook, as shown in Figure 2.24. To switch back to our original **Fruit** Workbook select **Window | 2 Fruit.xls** from the **Menu Bar** as shown in Figure 2.25.

caution!

The Windows Clipboard only stores one item at a time. Whenever you use the Edit | Paste Function, then whatever was last cut or copied to the Clipboard is pasted and this might not always be what you intended. Therefore you should consider Cut and Paste or Copy and Paste as a combined Function.

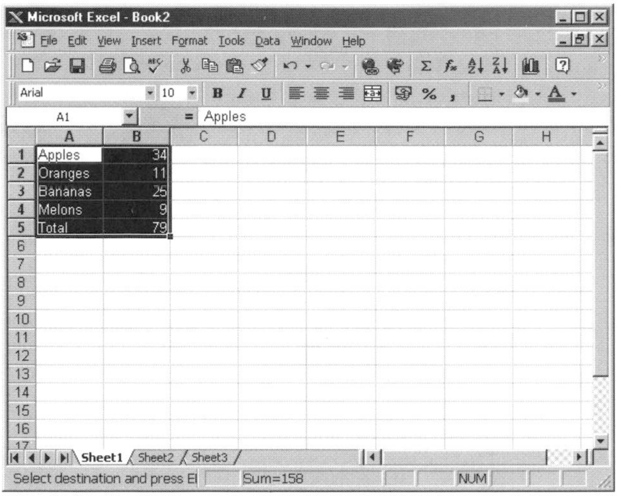

Figure 2.24 Copying between Workbooks.

Figure 2.25 Switching between Workbooks.

7. Now that we are back to our **Fruit** Workbook there is one final thing we can do in this section. Reselect cell range **B1:B5** as shown in Figure 2.26 and press the Delete key on the keyboard and the contents of the selected range will be deleted.

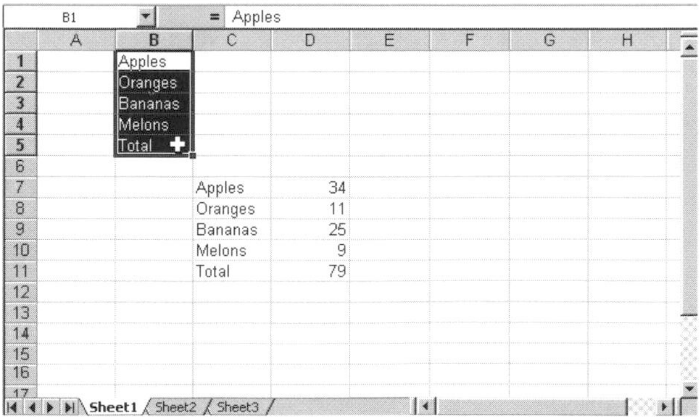

Figure 2.26 Deleting the contents of the selected range.

information

Whilst we can delete the contents of cells by selecting them and pressing the Delete key on the keyboard, we can achieve the same effect by simply omitting the Paste Function after performing an Edit I Cut operation.

step **8.** Finally, save the **Fruit** Workbook using **File I Save** on the **Menu Bar** and close Excel by choosing the **File I Exit** option on the **Menu Bar**. You will be prompted as to whether you wish to save the changes to **Book2** as shown in Figure 2.27 and you should select **No** in this instance as we don't need to keep this Workbook.

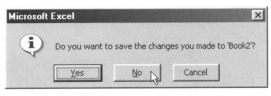

Figure 2.27 Prompt to save changes.

Summary

In this section we have seen how we can use the Windows Clipboard combined with Excel's Cut, Copy, and Paste Functions to copy, move, or delete the contents of spreadsheet cells both within a Worksheet or between Worksheets or Workbooks. You might like to practice these procedures so that you become more familiar with the principles involved.

2.4. Search and Replace

As data is entered into a spreadsheet it can become quite large and sometimes it can be difficult to find specific items. Fortunately Excel has some features that can make the task of finding information much easier than having to scroll through a large Worksheet.

In this section we will see how we can:

● Use the search command for specified cell content.
● Use the replace command for specified cell content.

Exercise 2.4

step**1.** If it is not already running start Excel and **Open** the **Fruit** Workbook. In order to make this exercise more effective we will start by copying the cell range **C7:D11** to a remote area of the Worksheet. Once selected and copied to the Clipboard, make cell **BX500** active and paste the contents of the Clipboard into this new position on the Worksheet, as in Figure 2.29. Use the scroll bars to see the full range of the pasted selection.

> **You can go quickly to a specific cell by using the Edit I Go To... option on the Menu Bar as in Figure 2.28. Here you can enter a cell Reference: and when you click on OK you will be positioned at the desired location.**

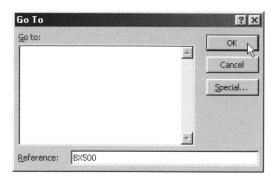

Figure 2.28 Using the Go To option.

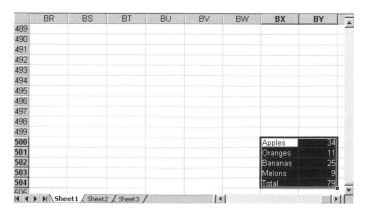

Figure 2.29 Selection pasted into cell BX500.

★ ECDL ★

2. Now, return to the previous position in the Worksheet by pressing the Home key whilst holding down the Ctrl key on the keyboard. This takes you back to make **A1** the active cell. Next, select **Edit | Find...** on the **Menu Bar** and the dialogue box shown in Figure 2.30 will be displayed.

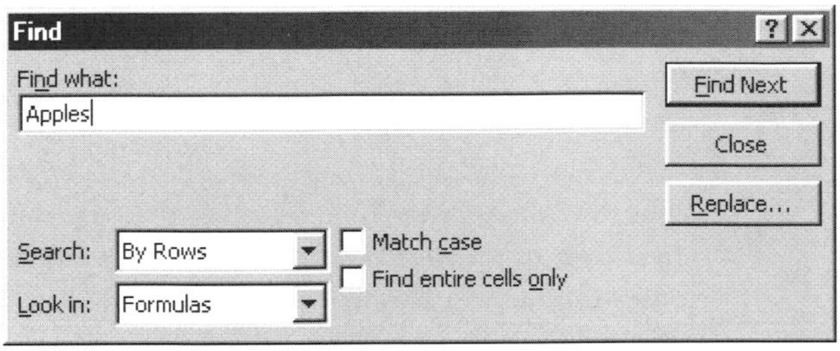

Figure 2.30 Using the Find option.

3. Type the word *Apples* in the **Find what:** box and click once on the **Find Next** button. Excel searches for the text string that you have entered and finds it first in cell **C7**. If you then click on the **Find Next** button, again Excel will look for the next occurrence of **Apples** in the Worksheet and it should find it in cell **BX500**. Note that the **Find** dialogue box stays on the screen until you close it.

4. Now return to cell **A1** and this time select the **Edit | Replace...** option on the **Menu Bar** and the dialogue box shown in Figure 2.31 will be displayed. We can use this option to replace the contents of a cell with something else. For example, in the **Find what:** box type the word *Melons* and in the **Replace with:** box type the word *Lemons*. Now you can choose whether you want Excel to replace all the occurrences of **Melons** with **Lemons** or just to replace the first occurrence that it finds. For this exercise we will change all **Melons** to **Lemons** so click on the **Replace All** button.

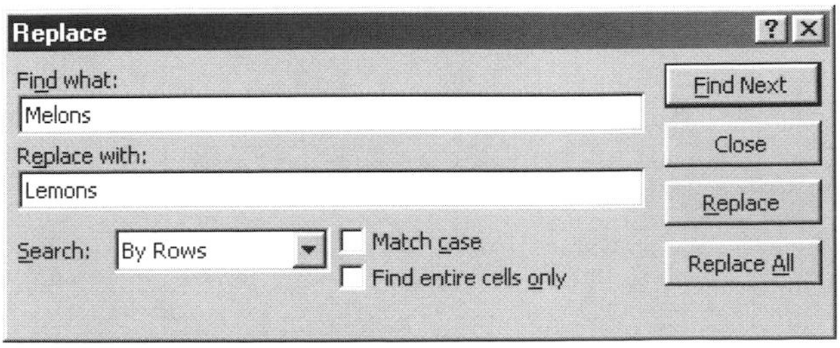

Figure 2.31 Using the Replace option.

step **5.** The **Replace** dialogue box will disappear and you will see that all the occurrences of **Melons** now read **Lemons**. Go to cell **BX503** and check it!

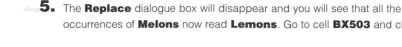

You can use the Edit I Replace... option to change Formulas as well as text stored in cells.

Summary

Both the Find and Replace options are extremely useful features of Excel especially when you are working with very large spreadsheets. Used wisely they can save you a considerable amount of time when you need to make repetitive changes to the contents of multiple cells.

2.5. Rows and Columns

We have seen previously how we can move the contents of cells by using the Copy, Cut, and Paste Functions in Excel. However, there is another way that we can move things around in a Worksheet by means of inserting or deleting selected rows or columns.

In this section we will see how we can:

● Insert rows and columns.
● Modify column width and row height.
● Delete selected rows or columns.

Exercise 2.5

step **1.** If it is not already running start Excel and Open the **Fruit** Workbook. Select row **11** and then click on **Insert I Row** on the **Menu Bar**. Notice how the original contents of row **11** are pushed downwards to become row **12** and a new blank row **11** has been inserted in the **Fruit** Worksheet as in the example in Figure 2.32.

	A	B	C	D	E	F	G	H	
1									
2									
3									
4									
5									
6									
7			Apples	34					
8			Oranges	11					
9			Bananas	25					
10			Lemons	9					
11									
12			Total	79					
13									
14									
15									
16									
17									

|◀ ◀ ▶ ▶|\Sheet1 / Sheet2 / Sheet3 /

Figure 2.32 Inserting a blank row.

2. We can perform a similar operation with columns. For example, select column **B** and click on **Insert | Column** on the **Menu Bar**. In this instance the contents of both columns **C** and **D** are shifted over to the right to make room for the newly inserted blank column as shown in Figure 2.33.

B1 ▼ =

	A	B	C	D	E	F	G	H	
1									
2									
3									
4									
5									
6									
7				Apples	34				
8				Oranges	11				
9				Bananas	25				
10				Lemons	9				
11									
12				Total	79				
13									
14									
15									
16									
17									

|◀ ◀ ▶ ▶|\Sheet1 / Sheet2 / Sheet3 /

Figure 2.33 Inserting columns.

shortcut

If you need to insert several additional rows then simply select multiple adjacent rows and then perform an Insert | Row operation. The equivalent number of new rows will be inserted into your Worksheet. The same applies to columns as well.

step **3.** So far we have only been entering a short amount of text in cells on our Worksheet but if we select cell **D12** and click on the **Formula Bar** we can add the word *amount* after the word *Total*, then press Return or click on the ✓ button to accept the change. Now you will see that the text is too wide to fit in the column as shown in Figure 2.34. Therefore we need to increase the width of the column to accommodate the extra letters.

Apples	34
Oranges	11
Bananas	25
Lemons	9
Total amou	79

Figure 2.34

step **4.** To increase the width of column **D** select the entire column and then click on the **Format I Column I Width...** option on the **Menu Bar**. A dialogue box as shown in Figure 2.35 will be displayed and if we enter a value of *12* and click on **OK** the width of column **D** will be increased accordingly. See the example in Figure 2.36.

Column Width	? X
Column width: 12	OK
	Cancel

Figure 2.35 Setting a column width.

C	D	E	F
	Apples	34	
	Oranges	11	
	Bananas	25	
	Lemons	9	
	Total amount	79	

Figure 2.36 Column D set to width 12.

5. We can perform a similar procedure with rows. For example, select row **12** and click on **Format I Row I Height...** on the **Menu Bar**. A dialogue box will display and you should enter a value of *25* and click on **OK** as in Figure 2.37. This time the height of row **12** is increased as shown in the example in Figure 2.38.

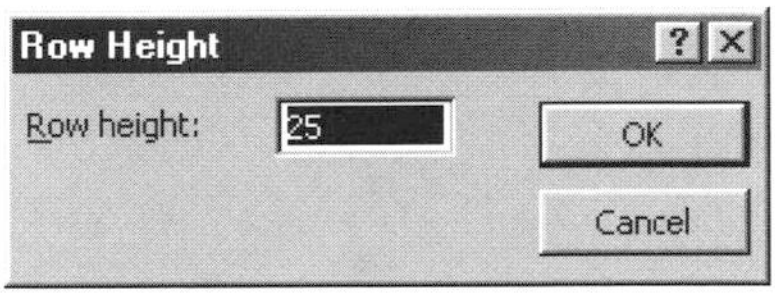

Row Height ? X

Row height: 25

OK

Cancel

Figure 2.37 Changing the row height.

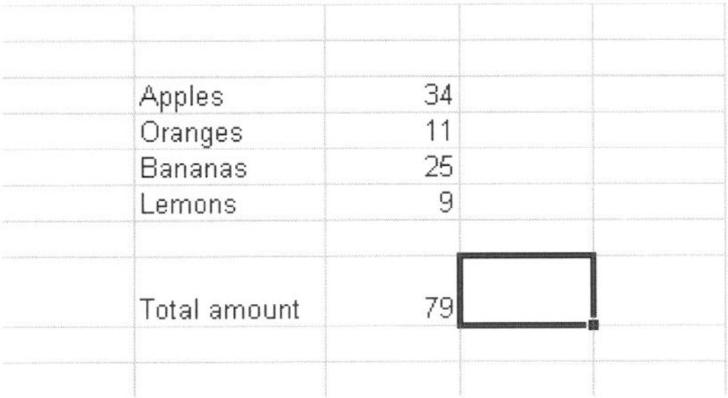

	Apples	34	
	Oranges	11	
	Bananas	25	
	Lemons	9	
	Total amount	79	

Figure 2.38 Row 12 increased to 25.

6. Previously in this section we have seen how rows and columns can be inserted into a Worksheet and the existing data will be automatically moved to accommodate the changes. The same principle applies when we delete a row or column, however there is one very important difference. When inserting rows or columns it doesn't matter whether there is any data already in the row or column selected but if you delete a row or column containing data then the data will be deleted along with the row or column itself. To see this in action select column **C** in our **Fruit** Worksheet and click on **Edit I Delete** on the **Menu Bar**. The data in the columns to the right of column **C** is shifted leftwards to take up the space vacated by the deleted column as shown in the example in Figure 2.39. Notice how the data that was originally in cells **D7:E12** is now in **C7:D12**.

	A	B	C	D	E	F
1						
2						
3						
4						
5						
6						
7			Apples	34		
8			Oranges	11		
9			Bananas	25		
10			Lemons	9		
11						
12			Total amount	79		
13						

Figure 2.39 The Fruit Worksheet after deleting column C.

step **7.** However, if we now select column **D** which contains the quantities of fruit and delete that column the data is also deleted as demonstrated in Figure 2.40. Either click on **Edit | Undo** or the **Undo** icon to reverse the column deletion action.

	A	B	C	D	E	F	G	H
1								
2								
3								
4								
5								
6								
7			Apples					
8			Oranges					
9			Bananas					
10			Lemons					
11								
12			Total amount					
13								
14								
15								
16								

Sheet1 / Sheet2 / Sheet3 /

Figure 2.40 Deleting columns or rows with data removes the data as well.

step **8.** Finally, Close the **Fruit** Worksheet saving any changes we have made so far.

Summary

Using row or column insert and delete operations is an ideal way of rearranging the data in a Worksheet. However, you may need to be careful when using row or column delete otherwise you might accidentally delete cell contents.

In this section we have also seen how we can alter the width of columns and the height of rows. This can be useful in helping to make a spreadsheet more readable.

2.6. Sort Data

When people enter data into a spreadsheet they frequently don't think too much about the order of things. Often, as in our Fruit example, items are entered in a fairly arbitrary way. However, sometimes it may be necessary to maintain a list of items in strict alphabetical or numerical order.

In this section we will see how this can be easily achieved and you will learn how to:

● Sort selected data in ascending or descending numeric order.
● Sort selected data in ascending or descending alphabetic order.

Exercise 2.6

1. Once again we will make use of our **Fruit** Worksheet. If it isn't already loaded then start Excel and **Open Fruit.xls** which should now look like Figure 2.41.

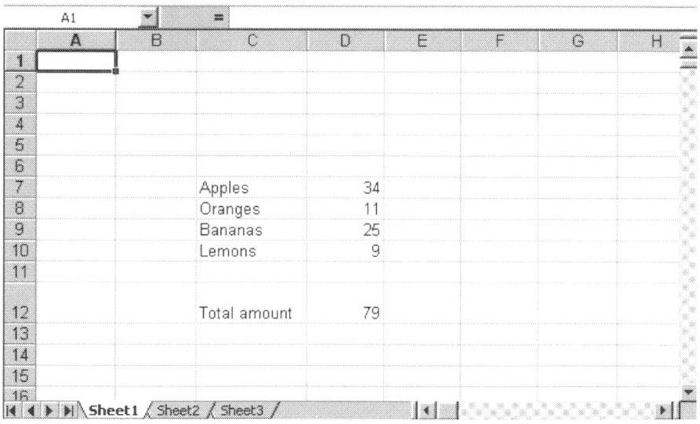

Figure 2.41 The Fruit Worksheet.

2. Start by selecting the cell range **D7:D10** and then click on **Data I Sort...** on the **Menu Bar**. A **Sort Warning** dialogue box will appear as shown in Figure 2.42 and this tells us that there is data alongside our selected range which we might wish to include in the sorting operation. For now we will ignore the labels next to the numbers and simply sort the numbers themselves, so select **Continue with current selection** and click on the **Sort...** button.

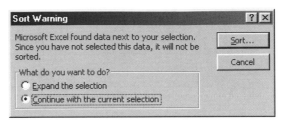

Figure 2.42 The Sort Warning dialogue box.

step **3.** Another dialogue box will now appear called Sort as shown in Figure 2.43. Here we can specify certain criteria for carrying out the sorting process but for now we will just accept the default settings and click on the **OK** button.

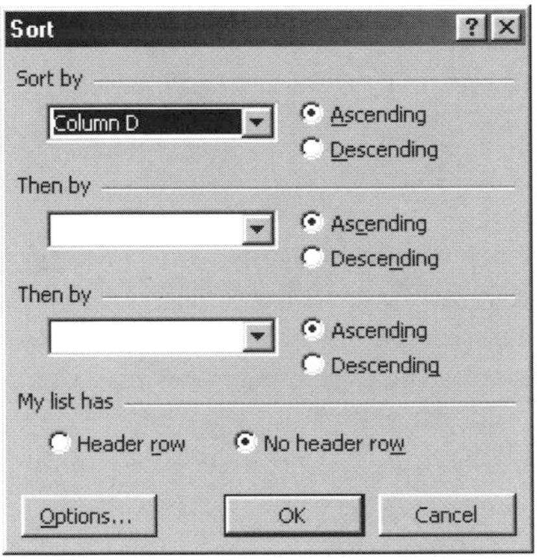

Figure 2.43 Setting the Sort criteria.

step **4.** The **Sort** dialogue box disappears and instantly the list of numbers has been sorted in ascending order as shown in Figure 2.44. Note: Once you have verified the fact that the numbers have been correctly sorted in ascending order, undo the sort operation by selecting **Edit | Undo** or by clicking once on the **Undo** ↰ icon on the **Standard** Toolbar.

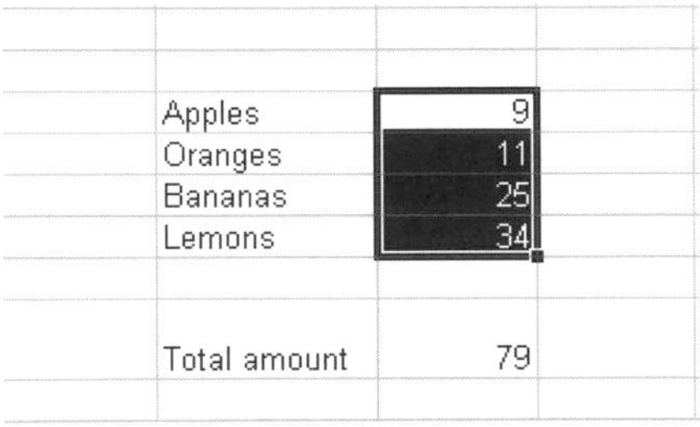

Figure 2.44 Numbers sorted in ascending order.

5. Next, we will sort the list of fruit into alphabetical order but this time we will include the quantities in the sorting operation. So, select the cell range **C7:D10** and click on **Data I Sort...** on the **Menu Bar**. Now you will notice that no **Sort Warning** dialogue box appears. On the **Sort criteria** window make sure that the sort is carried out on the fruit names by selecting **Column C** in the **Sort by** drop down list and then we can proceed with the sort by clicking on the **OK** button. Once again our selected range is sorted instantly with all the fruit and their associated quantities arranged in alphabetical order as shown in Figure 2.45.

Figure 2.45 The sorted list of fruit and quantities.

> **Instead of using the Data I Sort... option on the Menu Bar you can use the two Sort buttons on the Standard Toolbar, the Sort Ascending button and the Sort Descending button. However, when you use these buttons to perform a sort you will not be warned about any data in adjacent cells which you might wish to be included within the sort.**

> **When sorting multiple columns or rows the sorting order is dependant on the position of the cursor. Therefore when you click on either the Sort Ascending or Sort Descending icons on the Toolbar the sort operation will be carried out on the column or row that contains the cursor at the end of the selection process.**

6. Finally, **Close** the **Fruit** Workbook saving any changes that you have made.

Summary

By using the Sort facilities provided in Excel it is possible to completely rearrange the data stored in cells. This can be extremely useful if you need to maintain say a list of people's names in alphabetical order or sort a group of numbers into ascending or descending order of value. Most sorting within Excel takes place on columnar lists but you can also sort data in rows. In addition, the more advanced sorting features in Excel allow you to perform multi-level sorting, so for example you could sort a list of people by age in alphabetical order.

Review Questions

1. Approximately how many cells are there in a single Excel Worksheet?

2. Which keyboard character is used to define a contiguous range of cells in a Formula?

3. Which Menu Bar option would you use to reverse the last operation that you carried out?

4. How would you enter a series of numerical digits into a cell so that they are treated as text?

5. Which keyboard key do you need to use if you want to select a non-contiguous range of cells?

6. Whereabouts on the screen would you click with the mouse to select an entire:
a. Row?
b. Column?
c. Worksheet?

7. How many items can be stored in the Windows Clipboard at any one time?

8. What procedure would you use to:
a. Switch between Worksheets?
b. Switch between any open Workbooks?

9. Other than using the Delete key on the keyboard, how could you delete the contents of a range of cells?

10. What Menu Bar option would you use to move the active cell marker to a specific cell reference?

11. How would you increase the width of a Worksheet column?

12. Which tool icon on the Standard Toolbar would you use to sort a list of names into reverse alphabetical order?

Formulas and Functions

In this chapter you will learn how to

- *Use basic arithmetic and logical Formulas to perform a range of calculations.*
- *Use the AutoFill and Copy Handle tools to copy or increment data entries.*
- *Use relative and absolute cell referencing in Formulas or Functions.*
- *Use the COUNT and AVERAGE functions.*

We have already seen how you can use a Formula to perform a calculation based on the data stored in spreadsheet cells and as mentioned previously this is really the most useful feature of any spreadsheet package. However, so far we have only scratched at the surface when it comes to using Formulas in Excel and therefore we need to expand our knowledge in order to be able to produce more sophisticated and advanced spreadsheets.

As well as Formulas, Excel offers a range of Functions which can also be used to calculate and process spreadsheet data. Formulas and Functions work in slightly different ways so it is important to understand what they are and how they work.

definition

> **Formulas: A Formula is basically an equation that is used to analyse and process the data stored in a Worksheet. Formulas can perform very simple operations such as addition, multiplication, subtraction, and division, or they can be extremely complex using sophisticated mathematical, conditional and logical processing techniques to calculate their results.**

definition

> **Functions: Functions are predefined Formulas that perform calculations by using specific values, called arguments, in a particular order, known as the syntax. For example, the SUM Function adds values for ranges of cells where the range being totalled is the argument of the Function being performed. As with Formulas, Functions can be either simple or highly complex.**

Both Formulas and Functions can refer to other cells on the same Worksheet, cells on other sheets in the same Workbook, or cells on sheets in other Workbooks.

3.1. Arithmetic and Logical Formulas

In this section we will look at Formulas in more detail and you will learn how to:

- Use basic arithmetic and logical Formulas to perform a range of calculations in a spreadsheet e.g. addition, subtraction, multiplication, and division.
- Recognise standard error messages associated with Formulas.
- Use the AutoFill tool and Copy Handle tool to copy or increment data entries.
- Understand and use relative cell referencing in Formulas or Functions.
- Understand and use absolute cell referencing in Formulas or Functions.

Exercise 3.1

For this exercise we will start with a new blank Workbook.

step 1. If it is not loaded, then start Excel and a new blank Workbook will be created for us to work with. If Excel is already running then **Close** any open Workbooks and click on **File | New** on the **Menu Bar** or the **New** [ ] icon on the **Standard** Toolbar.

step 2. In our blank Worksheet enter the following data in the specified cells:

Cell reference	Value
B2	27
B3	49
B4	11
B5	19
C2	50
C3	22
C4	3
C5	6

step 3. Next, in cell **D2** type in the Formula =B2+C2 and press Return or Enter on the keyboard. In cell **D3** type in the Formula =B3-C3. In cell **D4** type in the Formula =B4*C4. And, finally, in cell **D5** type in the Formula =B5/C5. Your Worksheet should now look exactly like the example shown in Figure 3.1.

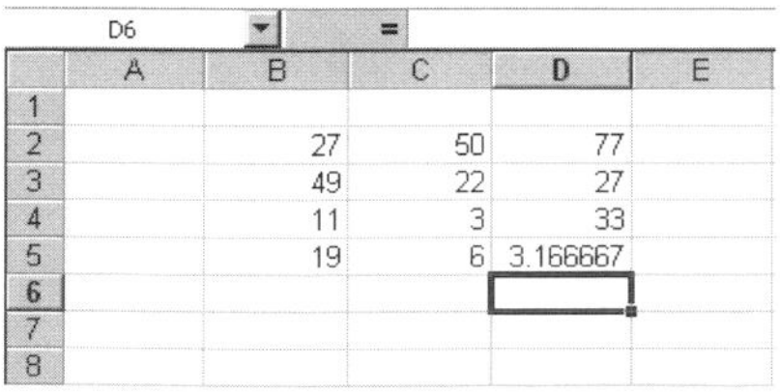

	A	B	C	D	E
1					
2		27	50	77	
3		49	22	27	
4		11	3	33	
5		19	6	3.166667	
6					
7					
8					

Figure 3.1 Simple arithmetic.

caution!

Notice how the result of dividing 19 by 6 in cell D5 is displayed as 3.166667, this is because by default Excel displays numbers to 15 digit precision but in this instance the column is not wide enough to display all of them and therefore the number is truncated to fit the space available.

step **4.** As well as actually typing cell references in Formulas we can use Excel to select them and automatically enter them into Formulas. For example, make cell **B6** active and type in an = sign. Now using either cursor control keys or the mouse, position the cell marker at **B2**. You will notice that the cell referenced (**B2**) now appears after the = sign in cell **B6**. Press the + sign key on the keyboard and then move to cell **B3**. Notice how a special cell marquee is used to highlight the cell you are selecting, see Figure 3.2. Press the + sign key again and then move to cell **B4**. Press the + once more and move to cell **B5**. Finally press the Return or Enter key and you will see that cell **B6** now contains the number **106** which is the result of **B2+B3+B4+B5** as per the Formula we have generated. Using this method of entering cell references into Formulas by pointing to them means that you are less likely to make mistakes when typing references in via the keyboard.

	A	B	C	D	E
1					
2		27	50	77	
3		49	22	27	
4		11	3	33	
5		19	6	3.166667	
6		=B2+B3			
7					
8					

SUM   X ✓ = =B2+B3

Figure 3.2 Entering a Formula by pointing to cell references.

information

Excel Formulas can contain 'constants', i.e. fixed values for use in calculations rather than just cell references. So, it is perfectly valid to enter a Formula such as =72*0.2 to calculate 20 percent of 72 giving the answer 14.4.

step **5.** Occasionally you may need to combine arithmetic Functions in a Formula in order to produce certain calculations. Here you must be aware that the order in which you enter mathematical symbols can effect the result of a calculation.

★ ECDL ★

For example, in cell **C6** enter the Formula =*C2-C3*C4* and Excel will calculate the result as **–16** because the multiplication is actually carried out before the subtraction, despite the fact that in the sum the – sign appears first. Basically, Excel uses an order of precedence when it comes to calculation. The order used is Division, Multiplication, Addition, then Subtraction. Therefore, if in our example we want Excel to perform the subtraction before the multiplication we have to use brackets in our Formula. Try this out by entering the Formula =*(C2-C3)*C4* into cell **C7**. You will now see that although we are referencing the same cells and using the same arithmetic operators the results are completely different with the new calculation using the brackets producing **84** as the result as shown in Figure 3.3.

C7	▼	▪	=(C2-C3)*C4	
	A	B	C	D	E
1					
2		27	50	77	
3		49	22	27	
4		11	3	33	
5		19	6	3.166667	
6		106	-16		
7			84		
8					
9					

Figure 3.3 Using brackets to change the calculation order within a Formula.

step **6.** When you enter a Formula Excel will check to see if it is syntactically correct. If it detects a mistake then an error value is generated. Error values can be the result of using text where a Formula expects a numeric value, deleting a cell that is referenced by a Formula, or using a cell that is not wide enough to display the result. For example, in cell **B8** on our Worksheet enter the Formula =*B6+I0* where what looks like the digit **1** is in fact a capital letter **i**, which is a common typing error. When you press the Return or Enter key an error is generated as shown in Figure 3.4. This is because we have mixed text in with numbers in our Formula and Excel cannot resolve the calculation.

B8	▼	▪	=B6+I0	
	A	B	C	D	E
1					
2		27	50	77	
3		49	22	27	
4		11	3	33	
5		19	6	3.166667	
6		106	-16		
7			84		
8		#NAME?			
9					

Figure 3.4 An error resulting from an invalid Formula being entered.

Some of the typical error values that you might encounter are as follows:

Error value	Typical cause
#NAME?	Text not recognised in a Formula.
#REF!	The cell being referenced is not valid.
#VALUE!	The wrong type of argument or operand is being used.
#NUM!	An error in a number used in a Formula.
#N/A	The value being used in a Formula is not available.
#NULL!	The two areas referenced do not intersect.
#########	The result calculated is too long to display in the cell.
#DIV/0	Division by zero not allowed.

shortcut

After encountering an error, if you don't fully understand what has caused it and how to rectify the problem use the Excel Help system to find more information about the error value displayed.

step **7.** **Close** the Workbook without saving the changes and then **Open** a new blank Workbook.

step **8.** On occasions you might need to enter the same value in a number of consecutive cells on a Worksheet. Whilst you could use **Copy** and **Paste** to do this, Excel has another feature called **AutoFill** which can prove useful and once mastered is much quicker. For example, on our new blank Worksheet enter the number *14* in cell **A1** and then select the cell range **A1:A6**. Now click on **Edit I Fill I Down** on the **Menu Bar**. Excel will automatically fill the range with the value entered in cell A1, as shown in Figure 3.5.

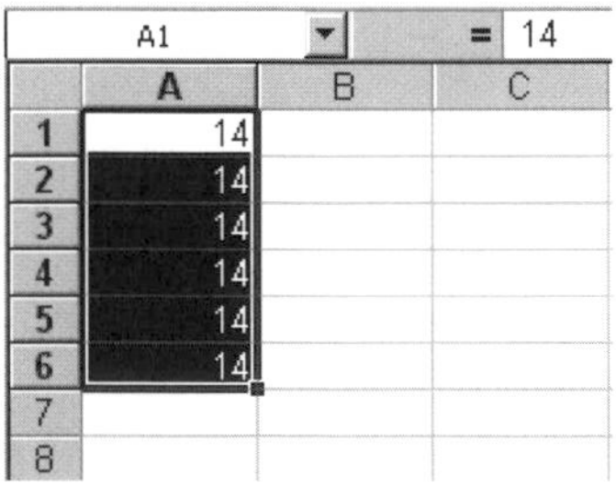

Figure 3.5 Filling a range of cells.

★ ★ ★
★ ★
★ ECDL ★
★ ★
★ ★ ★

> **You can use the Edit I Fill options to AutoFill a range of selected cells adjacent to the source cell in 4 different directions, Up, Down, Right or Left.**

9. Even quicker than using the **Edit I Fill I Down** option on the **Menu Bar** you can populate a range of cells with identical values using the mouse. For example, delete the contents of cells **A1:A6** and type the word *Grape* in cell **A1** and reposition the active cell marker at **A1**. Now, if you look carefully at the active cell marker you will see that there is a small black control handle in the bottom right hand corner called the **Fill Handle** as shown in Figure 3.6. (Note that this image has been magnified so that you can see the **Fill Handle** more easily.)

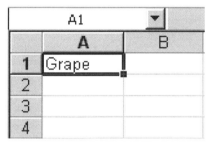

Figure 3.6 The Fill Handle.

10. Move the normal 🔁 pointer over the **Fill Handle** and it changes to a ✛ pointer. Now if you click on the **Fill Handle** and drag downwards with the mouse to **A6** as shown in Figure 3.7, when you release the mouse button the word **Grape** will fill the selected cells. Notice the small box showing you what will be placed in the target cells, this is useful when you are filling a large range and still cannot see the source cell on the screen.

Figure 3.7 Using the Fill Handle to AutoFill a range of cells.

step **11.** Whilst filling a range of cells with identical values is certainly useful from time to time, you are more likely to need to fill a range of cells with a group of consecutive values or a progressive series. For example, a product serial number or a list of employee numbers. Fortunately, Excel comes to our assistance once again with the AutoFill Series feature. Let's start by deleting the contents of the cell range **A1:A6** and entering the number *140020* in cell **B2**. This time we use the **Fill Handle** press and hold down the Ctrl key on the keyboard whilst dragging the mouse to cell **B7**. When you hold down the Ctrl key the ╋ pointer is supplemented by a tiny + sign like this ╋⁺ . As you drag the mouse downwards you will notice that the prompt box displays an increasing series of numbers as shown in Figure 3.8. When you release the mouse button and then the Ctrl key the cell range **B2:B7** is automatically filled with a series of consecutive numbers through to **140025** as shown in Figure 3.9.

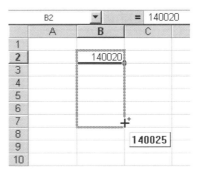

Figure 3.8 Using the Ctrl key to AutoFill a series of numbers.

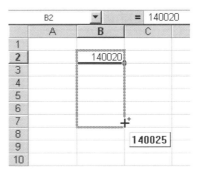

Figure 3.9 A simple number series created in a range of cells.

step **12.** We can also apply the Series feature to text and the most frequent use of this facility is when we wish to type in consecutive days of the week or months of the year. For example, delete the contents of the cell range **B2:B7** and type the word *Sunday* in cell **B2**. Now drag the **Fill Handle** to cell **H2** and when you release the mouse button you will see the other days of the week have been automatically entered into consecutive cells, as shown in Figure 3.10.

Figure 3.10 Using AutoFill to quickly enter the days of the week.

information

As well as using the mouse and the Fill Handle to AutoFill ranges you can use the Edit I Fill I Series... option on the Menu Bar. This displays a dialogue box as shown in Figure 3.11 where you can fine tune the way in which a series of cells is automatically filled.

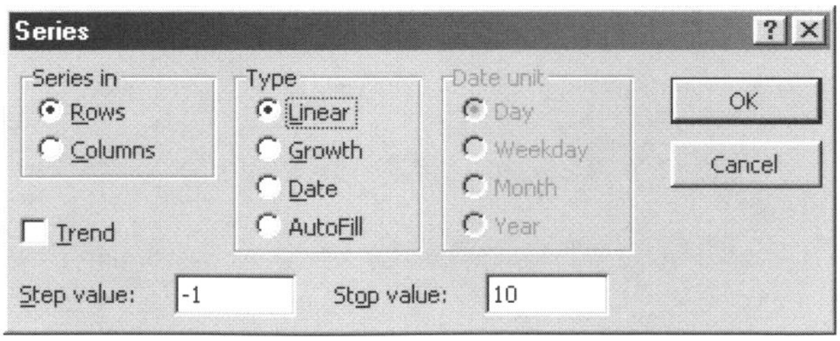

Figure 3.11 Defining how a series will be filled.

For example, you may wish to use a negative **Step value:** or to limit the **AutoFill** operation to a certain number of cells defined by the **Stop value:** box.

13. **Close** the Workbook without saving the changes and then **Open** a new blank Workbook.

14. So far, when we have been entering cell references in Formulas we have simply been typing things like *B2*, *C6:C10*, or *A1:D9*. This format is called Relative addressing and it means that when a Formula is copied across a range of cells, the Formula in each cell changes automatically to reflect the new source cells. In our blank Worksheet enter the following data in the specified cells.

Cell reference	Value
B2	45
B3	12
B4	62
C2	23
C3	l02
C4	19

15. Next, make cell **B5** the active cell and double click on the **AutoSum** Σ icon on the **Standard** Toolbar. This should result in the total **119** being displayed. Now, drag the **Fill Handle** to **AutoFill** cell **C5** and when you release the mouse button and select cell **C5** you will see that the Formula that has been copied has automatically adapted itself to refer to the range **C2:C4**, calculating the appropriate total of **144**, as shown in the **Formula Bar** in Figure 3.12.

C5	▼	=	=SUM(C2:C4)

	A	B	C	D
1				
2		45	23	
3		12	102	
4		62	19	
5		119	144	
6				
7				

Figure 3.12 An example of Relative addressing.

Normally, this action is precisely what we require Excel to achieve and on most occasions Relative addressing is the appropriate format to use.

16. However, sometimes we need to use a specific fixed cell reference in a range of Formulas. This can be done in Excel by using a technique known as Absolute addressing. As an example let's assume we wish to calculate the VAT on a range of values in cells.

17. **Close** the existing Workbook without saving the changes and then **Open** a new blank Workbook. In our blank Worksheet enter the following data in the specified cells:

Cell reference	Value
A1	0.175
B2	10
B3	60
B4	45.95
C2	B2*A1

18. Now, make cell **C2** the active cell and use the **Fill Handle** to **AutoFill** the cell range **C3:C4**. When you do this something strange happens. Instead of the new Formulas calculating the VAT the values of **0** have appeared. This is because the Formula in **C2** is using a Relative address for the reference to the VAT rate in cell **A1** and the cells **C3** and **C4** are referring to cells **A2** and **A3** respectively, which are empty. Hence, the wrong results have been produced as shown in Figure 3.13.

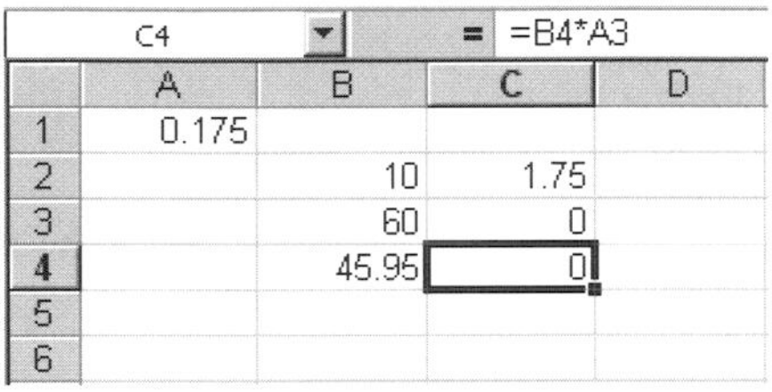

C4		▼	=	=B4*A3	
	A	B	C	D	
1	0.175				
2		10	1.75		
3		60	0		
4		45.95	0		
5					
6					

Figure 3.13 Incorrect VAT calculation.

19. We can correct this error by using Absolute addressing in the Formula in cell **C2**. To use an Absolute address we need to use $ signs in the cell reference. So, replace the Formula in cell **C2** with =B2*A1, this then refers to cell **A1** as an Absolute cell address. Now, when we use the **Fill Handle** to **AutoFill** cells **C3:C4** the correct VAT values are calculated, as shown in Figure 3.14.

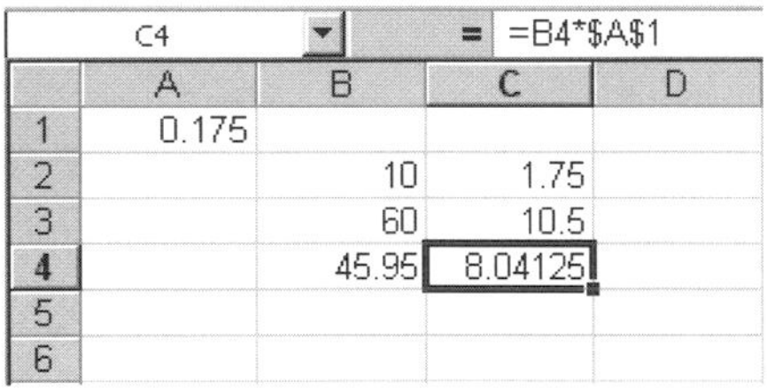

C4		▼	=	=B4*A1	
	A	B	C	D	
1	0.175				
2		10	1.75		
3		60	10.5		
4		45.95	8.04125		
5					
6					

Figure 3.14 Using Absolute addressing to perform a correct VAT calculation.

20. **Close** the existing Workbook without saving the changes.

shortcut

In our example VAT Worksheet we could simply put a
constant value in our Formula to calculate the VAT, like so
=B2*0.175. This would work perfectly well in most
circumstances but if the VAT rate changes we would need
to edit the Formulas in our spreadsheet. This is why we
have designated a specific cell which holds the value of
the current VAT rate and refer to it in our Formula. In this
way if the VAT rate changes we only have to change it in
one place in the spreadsheet. This is precisely why
Absolute addressing can be useful.

Summary

After completing this section you should now have an appreciation of
how important Formulas are when using a spreadsheet package like
Excel. In effect the use of Formulas is a bit like programming the
Worksheet, since once they have been entered correctly the
recalculation of their results is completely automatic. This is what
makes products like Excel so useful. When entering complex Formulas
it is quite easy to make mistakes and you should now understand
some of the types of error values that you may encounter in Excel. In
addition, we have seen how using the AutoFill facilities provided in
Excel can save an awful lot of time entering repetitive or serial data.

Lastly, in this section we have covered the differences between
Relative and Absolute addressing and seen why we might need to use
the different types of cell referencing within Formulas.

3.2. Working with Functions

As mentioned earlier, Functions are a type of in-built Formula that can
be used to perform calculations in a similar way to Formulas. Excel
provides a huge range of Functions both general purpose and more
specialist, covering areas such as engineering, statistics, finance,
mathematics, and trigonometry.

We have already covered the use of one of Excel's most commonly
used Functions – SUM – in Exercise 2.1, Step 7, so in this section we
will see how to:

● Use the COUNT Function.
● Use the AVERAGE Function.

★ ECDL ★

Exercise 3.2

step 1. If it is not loaded then start Excel and a new blank Workbook will be created for us to work with. If Excel is already running then **Close** any open Workbooks and create a new one.

step 2. In cell **B2** enter the number *1989* and then using the **AutoFill** feature generate a series of sequential numbers in the cell range **B3:B22** finishing with the number *2009*. Next, make cell **D10** the active cell and then select **Insert | Function...** on the **Menu Bar**. A dialogue box called **Paste Function** will appear as shown in Figure 3.15.

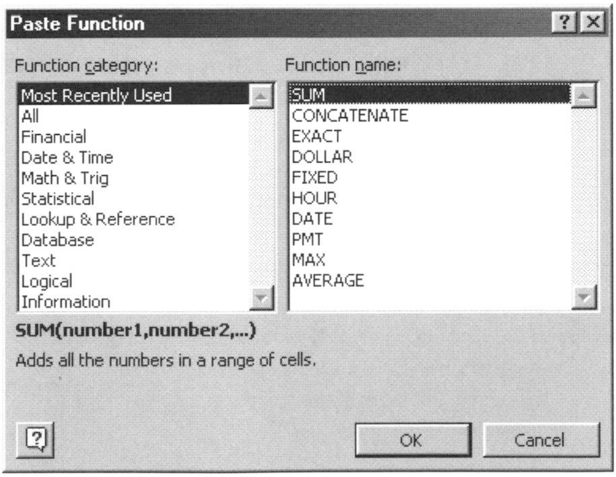

Figure 3.15 The Paste Function dialogue box.

step 3. Here we can select the specific Function that we want to use. On the left is a list of **Function categories** and on the right is a list of specific **Functions** within a category. By default Excel displays a list of the **Most Recently Used Functions**, assuming that we might want to use one of these again. However, the **COUNT** Function is not listed here so we need to select another category. The Function we need resides in the **Statistical** category so select this on the left and then using the scroll bar on the right hand box select the **COUNT** Function as shown in Figure 3.16.

Paste Function   **? X**

Function category: Function name:

Most Recently Used   AVERAGEA
All   BETADIST
Financial   BETAINV
Date & Time   BINOMDIST
Math & Trig   CHIDIST
Statistical   CHIINV
Lookup & Reference   CHITEST
Database   CONFIDENCE
Text   CORREL
Logical   COUNT
Information   COUNTA

COUNT(value1,value2,...)

Counts the number of cells that contain numbers and numbers within the list
of arguments.

[?]   OK   Cancel

Figure 3.16 Selecting the COUNT Function.

shortcut

**Instead of selecting Insert I Function... on the Menu Bar
you can click on the Paste Function icon on the Standard
Toolbar.**

step **4.** When you click on **OK** in the **Paste Function** box it disappears and a new
type of pop-up dialogue box appears in the top left hand corner of the
Worksheet as shown in Figure 3.17.

COUNT   ▼ X ✓ = =COUNT(B10:C10)

COUNT   H
        Value1 B10:C10   ▣ = {1997,0}
        Value2   ▣ = number
                                                       = 1
Counts the number of cells that contain numbers and numbers within the list of arguments.

        Value1: value1,value2,... are 1 to 30 arguments that can contain or refer to a
                   variety of different types of data, but only numbers are counted.

[?]   Formula result =1   OK   Cancel

10   1997   10:C10)
11   1998
12   1999

**Figure 3.17 Pop-up dialogue box which appears after
selecting Paste Function.**

step **5.** This window can now be used to enter the arguments for the **COUNT**
Function, so in the **Value1** box you should enter *B2.B22* and then click on
OK. The pop-up window will disappear and you will see that the cell **D10**
now contains the answer **21**, which is the number of items in the list **B2:B22**
as shown in Figure 3.18.

★ ECDL ★

	D10	▼	=	=COUNT(B2:B22)	
	A	B	C	**D**	E
1					
2		1989			
3		1990			
4		1991			
5		1992			
6		1993			
7		1994			
8		1995			
9		1996			
10		1997		21	
11		1998			
12		1999			
13		2000			
14		2001			
15		2002			
16		2003			
17		2004			
18		2005			
19		2006			
20		2007			
21		2008			
22		2009			
23					

Figure 3.18 The result of using the COUNT Function on the list of numbers.

shortcut

When using a pop-up window to enter the arguments for a Function you can use the mouse to select cells and ranges on the Worksheet itself rather than typing in cell references. However you might find that the pop-up window is obscuring the area of the Worksheet containing the cells you wish to select. If this is the case then you can move the pop-up window out of the way by clicking anywhere on the grey background and then dragging the window to a new position.

6. You might argue that counting a list of numbers is easy, especially as there are row numbers to help us. However, the **COUNT** Function can also be used to count the entries in any range of cells. For example, make a copy of **B2:B22** in both **A2:A22** and **C2:22**. Now, redefine the **COUNT** Function in **D10** so that the range being counted is *A2:C22* (you can do this by simply editing the **COUNT** Formula in the **Formula Bar** after selecting cell **D10**). You will see that the result of the **COUNT** Function is now **63** as shown in Figure 3.19.

D10	▼		■	=COUNT(A2:C22)	
	A	B	C	**D**	E
1					
2	1989	1989	1989		
3	1990	1990	1990		
4	1991	1991	1991		
5	1992	1992	1992		
6	1993	1993	1993		
7	1994	1994	1994		
8	1995	1995	1995		
9	1996	1996	1996		
10	1997	1997	1997	63	
11	1998	1998	1998		
12	1999	1999	1999		
13	2000	2000	2000		
14	2001	2001	2001		
15	2002	2002	2002		
16	2003	2003	2003		
17	2004	2004	2004		
18	2005	2005	2005		
19	2006	2006	2006		
20	2007	2007	2007		
21	2008	2008	2008		
22	2009	2009	2009		
23					

Figure 3.19 Using COUNT on a larger cell range.

step **7.** Next, delete the contents of cells **A5**, **A13**, **B8**, **B18**, **C3**, **C10**, and **C21**. Notice how the cell **D10** now shows the answer **56** as shown in Figure 3.20, this is because the **COUNT** Function will only count cells that contain numbers. Similarly, if a cell in a range being counted contains text it will be ignored.

D10	▼		■	=COUNT(A2:C22)	
	A	B	C	**D**	E
1					
2	1989	1989	1989		
3	1990	1990			
4	1991	1991	1991		
5		1992	1992		
6	1993	1993	1993		
7	1994	1994	1994		
8	1995		1995		
9	1996	1996	1996		
10	1997	1997		56	
11	1998	1998	1998		
12	1999	1999	1999		
13		2000	2000		
14	2001	2001	2001		
15	2002	2002	2002		
16	2003	2003	2003		
17	2004	2004	2004		
18	2005		2005		
19	2006	2006	2006		
20	2007	2007	2007		
21	2008	2008			
22	2009	2009	2009		
23					

Figure 3.20 Any gaps in the cell range will be ignored by the COUNT Function.

step 8. Finally, in our brief look at Functions we will use the **AVERAGE** Function to work out the average value of all the numbers in our range **A2:C22**. First, click on cell **D10** and delete the **COUNT** Function. Next, select **Insert** I **Function...** on the **Menu Bar** or click on the **Paste Function** f_x icon on the **Standard** Toolbar. On the **Paste Function** window select the **AVERAGE** Function (which is in the **Statistical** Functions category) and when the **AVERAGE** pop-up window appears enter the range *A2:C22* as shown in Figure 3.21 or select it using the mouse on the Worksheet area.

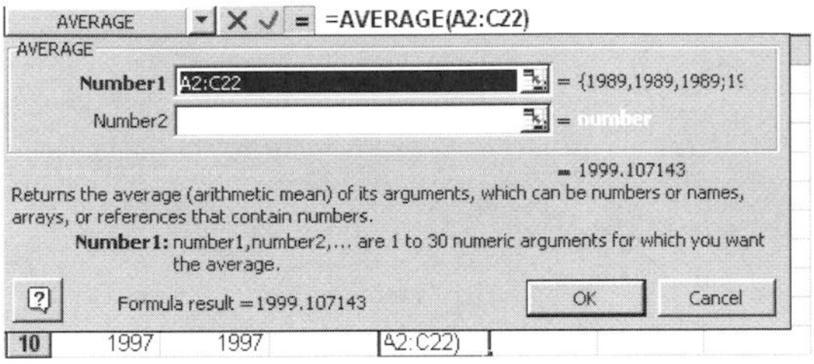

Figure 3.21 Using the AVERAGE Function.

step 9. After clicking on the **OK** button you will see that the average value of all the numbers in our selected list has been calculated as **1999.107** as shown in Figure 3.22. Notice how like the **COUNT** Function, the **AVERAGE** Function has ignored the cells without any numbers in them.

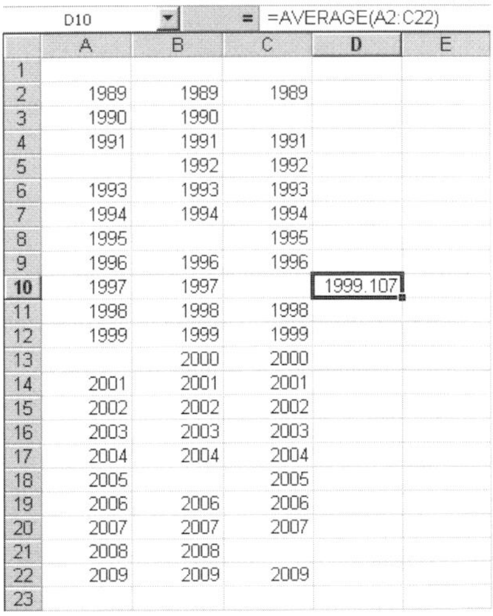

Figure 3.22 The result of using the AVERAGE Function on our range of cells.

step 10.Close the existing Workbook without saving the changes.

Summary

The Functions in Excel are even more powerful and sophisticated than the Formulas and as we have seen they can be put to very effective use. However, whilst Functions such as, SUM, COUNT, and AVERAGE are fairly easy to use, some of the more specialist Functions in Excel require a significant amount of in-depth knowledge in order to use them efficiently and correctly.

Review Questions

1. What is the difference between a Formula and a Function?

2. By default to how many digits of precision does Excel display numbers?

3. Which keyboard character is used to denote the start of a Formula or Function?

4. What order of precedence does Excel use when performing a calculation involving mixed arithmetical operators?

5. Why might you need to use brackets in a Formula?

6. What type of error causes #NAME? to be displayed when entering a Formula?

7. Which Menu Bar option would you use to automatically enter an identical value in a range of cells?

8. Which keyboard key would you hold down when using the mouse to populate a range of cells with a sequence of consecutive numbers?

9. What tool icon on the Standard Toolbar will automatically total numbers in a range of cells?

10. What is the difference between Relative Addressing and absolute addressing of cells?

11. In which Function category in the Paste Function dialogue box would you find the COUNT Function?

12. Which type of cells will be ignored by the AVERAGE Function?

Formatting

● *Format text and numerical data.*

● *Format ranges of cells.*

● *Use the spell checking tool.*

The ability to format various aspects of a spreadsheet can enable you to dramatically change its appearance. In fact some Excel Worksheets end up looking nothing like what you might perceive as a conventional spreadsheet. This is useful when you need to present the results of an analysis or calculation in say a formal report. You can change the format of a cell or range of cells using either the Format Menu or the Formatting Toolbar.

In this section you will learn how to do the following:

● Format Numerical Data.
● Format Text.
● Format Ranges of Cells.
● Check Spelling.

However, before we proceed further we need to create a new Workbook designed to produce invoices with a wide variety of data so that it can be used for the following exercises.

If it is not loaded then start Excel and a new blank Workbook will be created for us to work with. If Excel is already running then **Close** any open Workbooks and click on **File | New** on the **Menu Bar** or the **New** icon on the **Standard** Toolbar.

Next, enter the following data in the specified cells:

Cell reference	Value	
A1	Acme Trading Company	
A2	12 High Street	
A3	Newtown	
A4	Anywhere	
A5	ZZ9 9XX	
A7	Tel: 0119-989898	
A8	Fax: 0119-898989	
E1	A	
E2	C	
E3	M	
E4	E	
C10	Invoice	
A12	Customer:	
A13	A/C No:	
A14	Oder Date:	(Note that this is a deliberate mistake.)
A15	Invoice No:	

B12	Mr. Smith
B13	S001
B14	12/05/00
B15	5678
D12	Delivery Address:
D13	97 Main Road
D14	Fieldstone
D15	Yorkshire
D16	YY88 8WW
A19	Item Code
B19	Description
E19	Qty
F19	Unit Price
G19	VAT Rate
H19	VAT
I19	Item Total
A20	C001
A21	D005
A22	L089
A23	B012
B20	Chair
B21	Desk
B22	Lamp
B23	Catalogue
E20	2
E21	5
E22	1
E23	3
F20	5
F21	15
F22	10
F23	6.95
G20:G22	0.175
G23	0
H20	=(E20*F20)*G20
H21:H30	AutoFill from H20
I20	=(E20*F20)+H20
I21:I30	AutoFill from I20
H31	Total
I31	=SUM(I20:I30)

Once you have entered all the data detailed above, your spreadsheet should look like the example in Figure 4.1.

You should now **Save** the Workbook in the **My Documents** folder using the name *Invoice.xls*.

	A	B	C	D	E	F	G	H	I
1	Acme Trading Company Ltd.			A					
2	12 High Street			C					
3	Newtown			M					
4	Anywhere			E					
5	ZZ9 9XX								
6									
7	Tel: 0119-989898								
8	Fax: 0119-898989								
9									
10			Invoice						
11									
12	Customer:	Mr. Smith		Delivery Address:					
13	A/C No:	S001		97 Main Road					
14	Oder Date:	12/05/00		Fieldstone					
15	Invoice No:	5678		Yorkshire					
16				YY88 8WW					
17									
18									
19	Item Code	Description			Qty		Unit Price	VAT Rate	VAT	Item Total
20	C001	Chair			2		5	0.175	1.75	11.75
21	D005	Desk			5		15	0.175	13.125	88.125
22	L089	Lamp			1		10	0.175	1.75	11.75
23	B012	Catalogue			3		6.95	0	0	20.85
24									0	0
25									0	0
26									0	0
27									0	0
28									0	0
29									0	0
30									0	0
31									Total	132.475
32										

Sheet1 / Sheet2 / Sheet3 /

Figure 4.1 The Invoice.xls spreadsheet prior to formatting.

4.1. Format Cells – Numbers

Spreadsheet cells containing numbers or dates can be formatted in various ways in order to make them more understandable. For example:

- To display different number styles, such as number of decimal places, number of zeros after the decimal point, with or without commas to indicate thousands.
- To display different date styles.
- To display different currency symbols.
- To display numbers as percentages.

Exercise 4.1

For this exercise we will format the basic invoice which we created earlier so that it looks more professional and business like.

step **1.** If it is not loaded then start Excel and **Open** the Workbook **Invoice.xls**. Next, select cells **G20:G30**.

step **2.** Select the **Format | Cells...** option from the **Menu Bar**.

★ ECDL ★

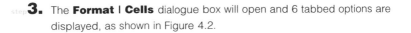
3. The **Format I Cells** dialogue box will open and 6 tabbed options are displayed, as shown in Figure 4.2.

Figure 4.2 The Format Cells dialogue box.

4. Next, click on the **Number** tab if it is not already selected and under **Category:** select **Number** – this allows you to change the way that numbers are displayed.

5. Now, make sure that the **Decimal places:** option is set to **2** and click **OK**.

6. The numbers in the selected range will now be displayed to 2 decimal places. Notice also in Figure 4.2 that there is a tick box labelled **Use 1000 Separator (,)** which can be used to ensure that large numbers are displayed with commas indicating the thousands.

shortcut

> **You can also switch the 1000 Separator in a cell or range of cells on and off by clicking on its icon on the Toolbar.**

7. Perform the same procedure on the range **H20:H31**.

8. Select cell **B14**.

9. Using the **Format I Cells** option (**Number** tab again) click on **Date** in the **Category:** list.

10. In the **Type:** list select **04-Mar-97** – this will format the date using the month name rather than the month number.

step**11.** Click on **OK**.

> **Excel allows you to format dates in a variety of different styles. For example 4/3/97 can be displayed as 04/03/97, 04/03/1997, 4-Mar-97, 04-Mar-97, 4-Mar, Mar-97, March-97 or March 4, 1997 depending on which Type you choose in the Format Cells I Number tab dialog box.**

step**12.** Select cell **I31**.

step**13.** Using the **Format I Cells** option (**Number** tab again) click on **Currency** in the **Category:** list.

step**14.** Next, in the **Symbol:** list select the desired currency character (**£**, **$, DM**, etc.).

step**15.** Click on **OK**.

> **Formatting numbers as currency is a frequent requirement. There is a Currency icon on the Toolbar which you can use to quickly format any selected range of numbers to be displayed using the default currency settings.**

step**16.** Finally, select cells **G20:G30**.

step**17.** Using the **Format I Cells** option (**Number** tab again) click on **Percentage** in the **Category:** list.

step**18.** Set the number of **Decimal places:** to *1* – this will format the VAT Rate cells as percentages with a single decimal place.

step**19.** Click on **OK** and your **Invoice.xls** Worksheet should now look like the example in Figure 4.3.

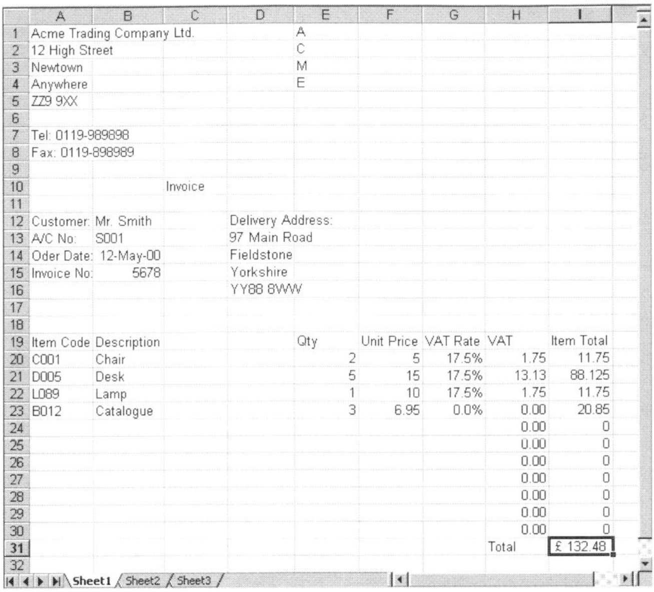

Figure 4.3 Invoice.xls after formatting numbers.

20. Select **File I Save** on the **Menu Bar** or click on the **Save** 🖫 icon to save the changes we have made so far.

4.2. Format Cells – Text

The text data in a spreadsheet can be formatted in a similar way to how text is formatted in a word processing document. Formatting is frequently used for column headings and labels. Different types of formatting can be used to emphasise text or to make it more readable. For example:

● Using bold, italic, or different font types.
● Using different text font colours.
● Using various text orientations.

Exercise 4.2

For this exercise we will continue formatting our invoice to make it even more presentable.

1. If it is not already loaded then **Open** the Workbook **Invoice.xls**.

2. Select cells **A19:I19**.

3. Select **Format I Cells...** from the **Menu Bar**.

step **4.** Click on the **Font** tab if it is not already selected – this allows you to change the way that the selected text is displayed, also referred to as the text attributes, as shown in Figure 4.4.

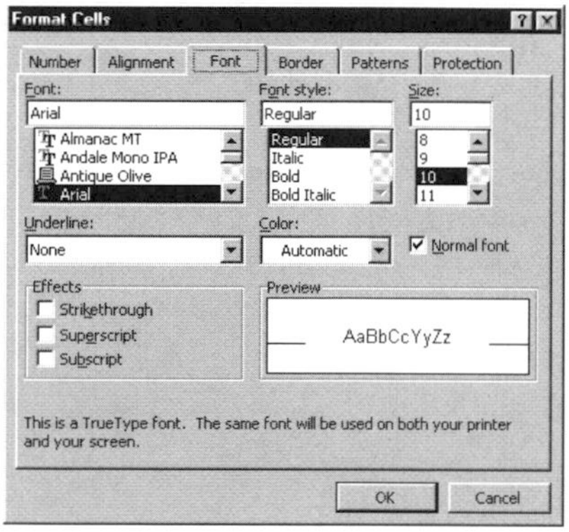

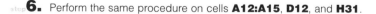

Figure 4.4 The Format Cells | Font tab.

definition

Text Attributes: Text consists of a font, point size, and a style e.g. Arial font, 16 point, bold, italic, underline. Each of these settings is called an attribute and you can use them to alter the way that text appears both on the screen and when it is printed out.

step **5.** Under the **Font style:** list select **Bold Italic** and click on **OK** – the column headings will now be emphasised and stand out from the remaining text.

shortcut

The Formatting Toolbar can be used to quickly change text attributes. Simply select the target cells and click on the appropriate icons on the Toolbar.

step **6.** Perform the same procedure on cells **A12:A15**, **D12**, and **H31**.

step **7.** Now it's time for a little colour. Select cells **A1:A8** and click on the **Color:** list on the **Font** tab in the **Format | Cells...** menu option. You can choose any of the colours listed and the text will change accordingly.

step **8.** Perform the same procedures on cells **C10** and **E1:E4**.

As well as changing the font colour you can also change the background colour of selected cells by selecting the Patterns tab. In addition, shading patterns can be used to create some very effective colour schemes.

Certain combinations of font and background colours can produce text that is very difficult to read. In fact it is possible to set both the font and the background to the same colour so that the text is effectively invisible!

9. Lastly in this exercise we will change the orientation of some text. Select cells **E1:E4** and open the **Format I Cells...** option on the **Menu Bar** again.

10. Click on the **Alignment** tab and on the right you will see the **Orientation** control, as shown in Figure 4.5.

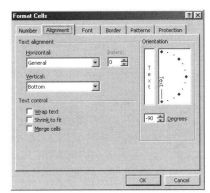

Figure 4.5 Changing the alignment of text.

11. Click on the red diamond at the end of the pointer and drag it downwards so that the **Degrees** indicator shows **–90** and release the mouse button.

12. Click on **OK** and the text spelling out the word **ACME** should now appear on its side, as shown in Figure 4.6. (Note that you cannot see the actual colours used in this formatting example but you should notice that the coloured areas are slightly lighter.)

	A	B	C	D	E	F	G	H	I	
1	Acme Trading Company Ltd.				A					
2	12 High Street				C					
3	Newtown				M					
4	Anywhere				E					
5	ZZ9 9XX									
6										
7	Tel. 0119-989898									
8	Fax. 0119-898989									
9										
10			Invoice							
11										
12	*Customer:* Mr. Smith			*Delivery Address:*						
13	*A/C No:* S001			97 Main Road						
14	*Oder Date* 12-May-00			Fieldstone						
15	*Invoice N* 5678			Yorkshire						
16				YY88 8WW						
17										
18										
19	*Item Code* *Description*				*Qty*	*Unit Price*	*VAT Rate*	*VAT*	*Item Total*	
20	C001	Chair			2	5	17.5%	1.75	11.75	
21	D005	Desk			5	15	17.5%	13.13	88.125	
22	L089	Lamp			1	10	17.5%	1.75	11.75	
23	B012	Catalogue			3	6.95	0.0%	0.00	20.85	
24								0.00	0	
25								0.00	0	
26								0.00	0	
27								0.00	0	
28								0.00	0	
29								0.00	0	
30								0.00	0	
31							*Total*	£ 132.48		
32										

Sheet1 / Sheet2 / Sheet3 /

Figure 4.6 The Invoice.xls Worksheet after formatting the text.

step **13.** You might want to apply some other attributes such as colour, pattern and point size to make this section of the spreadsheet appear like a company logo.

step **14.** Once again select **File I Save** on the **Menu Bar** or click on the **Save** 💾 icon to save the changes we have made so far.

information

> **Changing the orientation of text within cells is a useful way of reducing the width of columns where the heading is much longer than the data being stored. Simply align the text vertically and it will take up less column width.**

4.3. Format Cells – Cell Ranges

When you enter text into cells it is aligned towards the left by default. Numbers on the other hand are by default aligned to the right within cells. However, you can change the alignment of data within cells both horizontally and vertically. You can also format ranges of cells in other ways. For example:

● Centre and align cell contents in a selected cell range: left and right; top and bottom.

● Add border effects to a selected cell range.

★ ECDL ★

Exercise 4.3

Once again we will continue to smarten up our invoice.

1. Open the Workbook **Invoice.xls** if it is not already loaded.

2. Select column **A** and open the **Format I Column I Width...** menu option and the dialogue box shown in Figure 4.7 should be displayed.

Column Width	? X
Column width: 9.43	OK
	Cancel

Figure 4.7 Formatting the column width

3. Set the width of column **A** to *16* and click on **OK**.

4. Select cells **A12:A15** and open the **Format I Cells...** menu option again.

5. Click on the **Alignment** tab and in the **Horizontal:** list select **Right**, then click on **OK**. The text in these cells will now be aligned towards the right hand side of the column. However, whilst the adjacent text in cells **B12:B13** now looks fine, the date in cell **B14** and the number in cell **B15** look decidedly misplaced.

6. Select cells **B14:B15** and align them both to the left using the procedure above but selecting **Left** in the **Horizontal:** list.

7. Cells **A12:B15** in your spreadsheet should now look like Figure 4.8.

11		
12	*Customer:*	Mr. Smith
13	*A/C No:*	S001
14	*Oder Date:*	12-May-00
15	*Invoice No:*	5678
16		

Figure 4.8 Aligning cells.

8. Next, select row **19** and click on the **Centre** ≣ icon on the **Formatting** Toolbar. This will align the column headings text centrally within their cells.

9. The cell contents in a selected cell range can also be aligned vertically. Select cell **C10** and increase the font size to *20*. Notice how the height of the row is increased automatically to accommodate the new point size. Now increase the height of the row to *50* by using the **Format | Column | Height...** menu option. Notice how the text is aligned towards the bottom of the cell.

10. Once again select cell **C10** and open the **Format | Cells...** menu option. Click on the **Alignment** tab and from the **Vertical:** list select **Center** and click on **OK**. The word **Invoice** will now be neatly central within the row height, as in Figure 4.9.

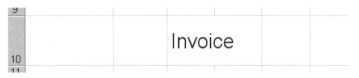

Figure 4.9 Vertical alignment within a cell.

shortcut

Adjusting the width of columns and the height of rows can be achieved more quickly and easily by moving the appropriate column or row boundary using the mouse. When you position the mouse cursor over a column boundary, clicking and dragging allows you to adjust the boundary width, as shown in Figure 4.10.

Figure 4.10 Adjusting a column width using the mouse.

To make the column width fit the contents, double-click the boundary to the right of the column heading, or to make a row fit the contents double-click the boundary at the bottom on the desired row.

11. Our last bit of tidying up involves formatting the borders of the ranges of cells. Select cells **A19:I30** and click the **down** arrow next to the **Borders** button (Figure 4.11) on the **Formatting** Toolbar which will display a drop down list

(Figure 4.12). Select the second from the left on the bottom row and you will see the selected cells now have borders around them, as shown in Figure 4.13.

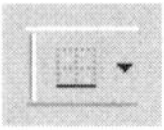

Figure 4.11 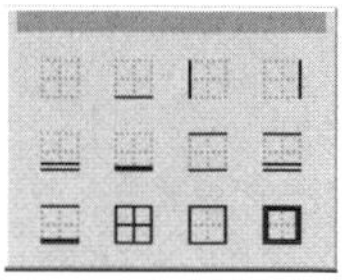   **Figure 4.12**

19	Item Code	Description		Qty	Unit Price	VAT Rate	VAT	Item Total
20	C001	Chair		2	5	17.5%	1.75	11.75
21	D005	Desk		5	15	17.5%	13.13	88.125
22	L089	Lamp		1	10	17.5%	1.75	11.75
23	B012	Catalogue		3	6.95	0.0%	0.00	20.85
24							0.00	0
25							0.00	0
26							0.00	0
27							0.00	0
28							0.00	0
29							0.00	0
30							0.00	0
31							Total	£ 132.48

Figure 4.13 Thin borders round cells.

12. Next, select cells **H31:I31** and this time select the bottom right hand corner border option. The **Totals** cells now have a thicker border around them as in Figure 4.14.

		0.00	0
	Total	£ 132.48	

Figure 4.14 Thick borders round cells.

13. Whilst the **Border** tool on the **Formatting** Toolbar provides a quick and easy way to add or remove borders to a range of cells, its options are fairly limited. The **Border** tab on the menu option is far more powerful and flexible.

14. Select cells **D12:F17**, select **Format I Cells...** and choose the **Border** tab.

15. Click on the double line in the **Line I Style:** list and then click on the **Outline** button. This will create a double lined border around the **Delivery Address** box on our invoice, as shown in the preview box.

16. Now click on the thick line just above the double line in the **Line I Style:** list and then click on the **Top Border** button which is next to the top left hand corner of the preview box. Click on **OK** and the **Delivery Address** box on your invoice should appear like Figure 4.15. Meanwhile the complete **Invoice.xls** Worksheet should now look like the example in Figure 4.16.

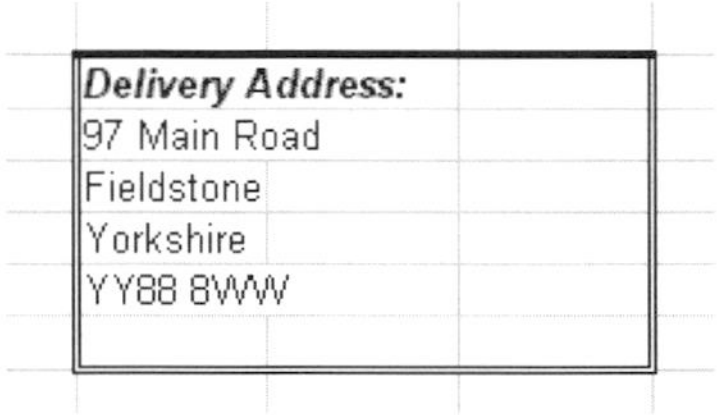

Figure 4.15 Formatting of the Delivery Address: box.

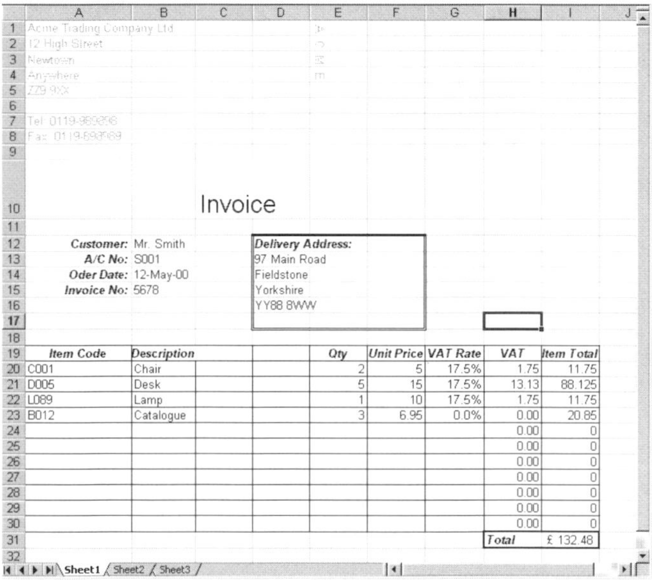

Item Code	Description			Qty	Unit Price	VAT Rate	VAT	Item Total
C001	Chair			2	5	17.5%	1.75	11.75
D005	Desk			5	15	17.5%	13.13	88.125
L089	Lamp			1	10	17.5%	1.75	11.75
B012	Catalogue			3	6.95	0.0%	0.00	20.85
							0.00	0
							0.00	0
							0.00	0
							0.00	0
							0.00	0
							0.00	0
							0.00	0
							Total	£ 132.48

Figure 4.16 The Invoice.xls Worksheet after formatting various cell ranges.

step **17.** Once again select **File | Save** on the **Menu Bar** or click on the **Save** icon to save the changes we have made so far.

4.4. Spelling

Just as when using a word processor to produce documents it is important to ensure that all the words in a spreadsheet are spelt correctly if you are to create a good impression. Therefore we need to:

● Use a spell-check program and make changes where necessary.

Exercise 4.4

1. If it is not already open, then **Open** the Workbook **Invoice.xls**.

2. Excel has a spelling checker which can be activated by either clicking on the ✓ button on the **Standard** Toolbar or selecting **Tools I Spelling...** from the menu options.

3. When triggered the Spelling checker option will check the entire spreadsheet or the currently selected range of cells. Therefore if you want to check the whole of the spreadsheet make sure that the active cell is **A1**.

4. When the Spelling checker encounters what it thinks is an incorrectly spelt word it highlights the cell and displays a dialogue box, as in Figure 4.17.

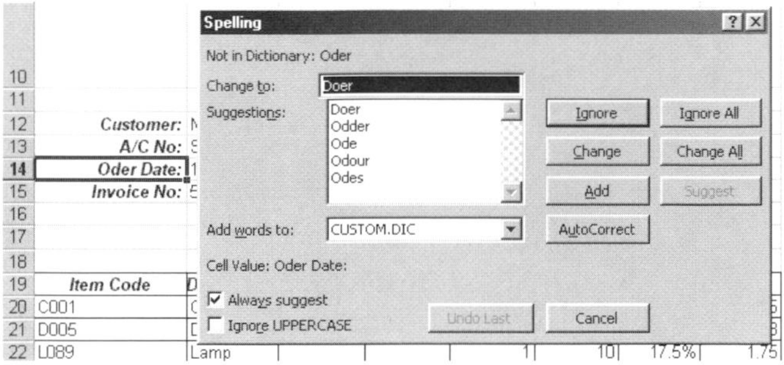

Figure 4.17 The Spelling checker in action.

5. In the example above you can see that the word **Order** has been typed in as *Oder* and the Spelling checker has presented a list of suggested corrections. If the correct spelling is listed as a suggestion you can simply double-click on it to accept it. However, in this particular case the correct word (**Order**) has not been suggested, in which case you can simply type the correct spelling in the **Change to:** box and then click on the **Change** button.

6. If the word is not found in the dictionary but you know that it is spelt correctly you can click on the **Ignore** button (or **Ignore All** button if there is likely to be more than one occurrence of the word).

step **7.** When you either **Change** or **Ignore** an incorrectly spelt word the Spelling checker will then move on to search for the next possible incorrect word in the spreadsheet.

step **8.** Save any changes made to the Workbook.

Summary

In this chapter we have covered the various ways that certain elements within a spreadsheet can be formatted as a means of enhancing its appearance. Both numbers and text can be altered to produce different effects and you can often apply formatting options to a range of cells. In addition, spelling and the way a spreadsheet is presented on the printed page have also been covered as formatting features.

As you can now appreciate there are numerous options and choices regarding how you can format a spreadsheet and with a little practice you can produce some really professional looking results.

Review Questions

1. How can you specify the number of decimal places a value in a cell should display?

2. Which Menu Bar option would you use to display a number in a cell as a monetary amount?

3. What is a text attribute?

4. Why do you sometimes need to be careful when changing text fonts and cell background colours?

5. What procedure would you use to produce vertical text in a cell?

6. What happens to the row height when you increase the font size of text in a cell?

7. The Border tool has limited choices so what Menu Bar option will provide better control over cell borders?

8. When using the Spelling check tool what choices are you given when it finds an incorrectly spelt word?

5

Printing

- *Modify the margin settings of a spreadsheet document.*
- *Change the document orientation.*
- *Adjust the document setup to fit on one page.*
- *Add a Header and Footer.*
- *Select the appropriate basic print options.*
- *Use the Print Preview tool prior to printing a spreadsheet.*
- *Print a Worksheet or Workbook.*
- *Print part of a Worksheet or a pre-defined cell range.*

5.1. Document Setup

Before we move on to actually printing our invoice it is important to understand how we can control the way that a spreadsheet is printed. In this section you will learn how to:

● Setup documents for printing.
● Modify document margin settings.
● Change document orientation, specifying portrait or landscape, page size etc.
● Adjust document setup to fit one page.
● Add a Header and Footer.

Exercise 5.1

Margins are used to control the blank borders around a printed spreadsheet on the page. They can be adjusted so that the data printed is positioned neatly on the page and frequently you may need to reduce the margins so that more of a spreadsheet can be printed on a page.

step**1.** If it is not already open, then **Open** the Workbook **Invoice.xls**.

step**2.** Next, select **File I Page Setup...** from the menu options and then select the **Margins** tab, as shown in Figure 5.1.

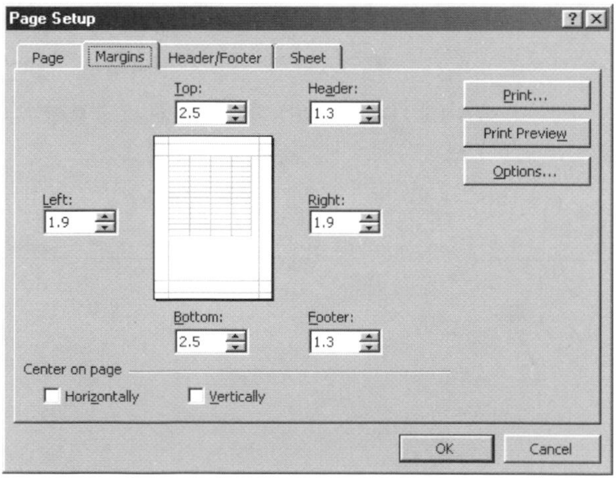

Figure 5.1 The Page Setup dialogue box.

step**3.** You can adjust the various margin settings by typing in new values (in cms) or by using the control to increase or decrease the values. You need to click on the **Print Preview** button in order to see the results of any changes that you make.

shortcut

The are two check boxes on the Margins tab under where it says "Center on page", these are labelled **Horizontally** and **Vertically**. If you select these then the printed data will be automatically centred on the page for you.

4. Now click on the **Page** tab as shown in Figure 5.2. Here you can set the **Orientation** of the printed page as either **Portrait** (this is the default) or **Landscape**. Because many spreadsheets are often wider than they are long printing them out in Landscape format is a useful feature of Excel.

Figure 5.2 Switching between Portrait and Landscape printing.

5. Just below the **Orientation** section on the **Page** tab there is a section called **Scaling**, as shown in Figure 5.3. These settings can be used to adjust the size of the print on the paper. For example you can increase or shrink the print by a percentage using the **Adjust to:** control, or force the print to fit on a specific number of pages using the **Fit to:** controls. Also on the **Page** tab there are boxes to select the **Paper size:** and the **Print quality:** you want to use. However, the settings available in these two drop down lists depend on the type and model of printer that you are using.

Figure 5.3 Adjusting the scale of the print.

step **6.** Next, select the **Header/Footer** tab on the **Page Setup** dialogue box, as shown in Figure 5.4.

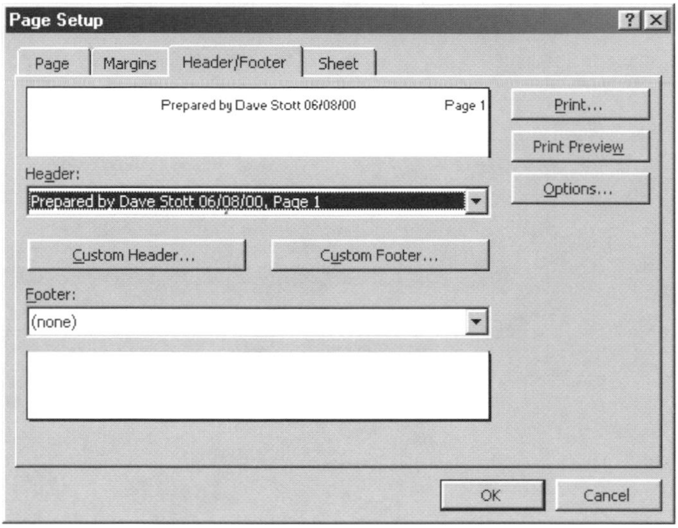

Figure 5.4 Setting up the Headers and Footers for a Worksheet.

step **7.** Headers and Footers can be printed automatically on every page generated when you print out your spreadsheet. This is very useful when a spreadsheet spans several pages. On this tab there are a selection of predefined Headers and Footers that you can choose, or you can define your own by clicking on the **Custom Header...** or **Custom Footer...** buttons, as shown in Figure 5.5.

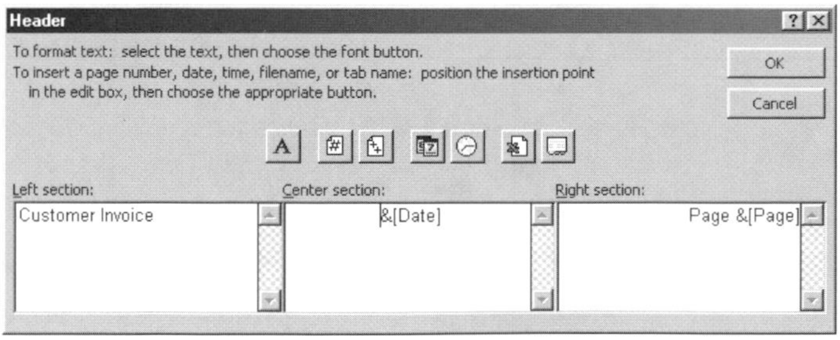

Figure 5.5 Specifying a Custom Header.

96

step **8.** Once again you can click on the **Print Preview** button to see the effects of any changes that you have made.

step **9.** Save any changes made to the **Invoice.xls** Workbook.

5.2. Printing Simple Spreadsheet Documents

Now that we have performed the document setup procedures we can actually start to think about printing our invoice. In this section we will learn how to:

● Use basic print options.
● Preview a spreadsheet.
● Print a Worksheet or a Workbook.
● Print part of a Worksheet or a pre-defined cell range.

Exercise 5.2

step **1.** Once again, if it is not already open then **Open** the Workbook **Invoice.xls**.

step **2.** Select the option **File I Print...** on the **Menu Bar** and a **Print** dialogue box like the one shown in Figure 5.6 will appear. This dialogue box can be used to control the actual printing of a Worksheet. At the top you can select the specific **Printer** that you want to use for this particular print job (normally the current Windows default printer is shown here). There is a **Properties** button that displays the selected printer settings which you can alter. Note that the actual printers available in the drop down list will depend on what printers have been installed in your Windows system. In the **Print range** section you can define how much of the Worksheet is to be printed by selecting **All** or a range of Page(s). The **Copies** section lets you print multiple copies of a print job and to **Collate** (assemble in order) the copies if you wish. Finally, on the **Print** dialogue box there is a section labelled **Print what**. Here you can specify whether you want to print a **Worksheet Selection**, the current **Active sheet(s)**, or the **Entire Workbook**. Once you are satisfied with the various settings controlling the print job simply click on the **OK** button to start the printing process.

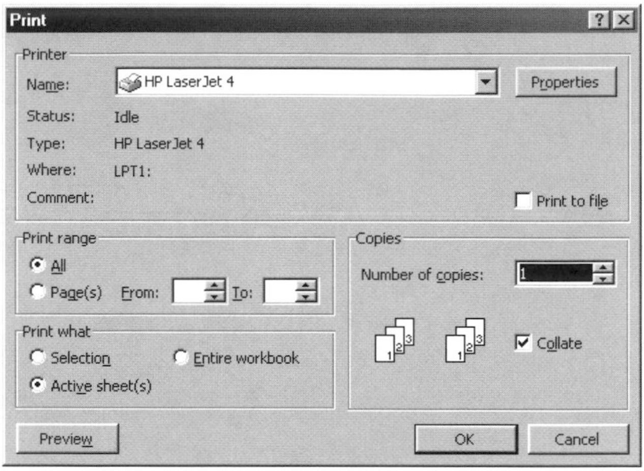

Print	? ☒

Printer

Name: 📇 HP LaserJet 4 ▼ | Properties

Status: Idle
Type: HP LaserJet 4
Where: LPT1:
Comment: ☐ Print to file

Print range
⊙ All
○ Page(s) From: [   ] 🔼 To: [   ] 🔼

Print what
○ Selection   ○ Entire workbook
⊙ Active sheet(s)

Copies
Number of copies: [1   ] 🔼

☑ Collate

Preview | OK | Cancel

Figure 5.6 Controlling a print job.

Instead of using the File I Print... option from the Menu Bar you can simply click on the Print icon on the Standard Toolbar. However if you do this then you forego the opportunity of changing any Print settings and the printout will be produced using the default settings, which are: the current default Windows printer, print All pages, print 1 Copy, and print the Active sheet(s).

Assuming you are using A4 paper and that you print using the default settings, then when you print the Invoice.xls Worksheet it is likely to print on two pages, with the Item Total column on the second page. This is because the Invoice is too wide to fit on a single sheet of A4 in Portrait format. Therefore if you experience this problem simply select Landscape Orientation on the Page Setup I Page tab and print the document again.

3. Before you actually produce any printed pages you can, if you wish, look at a Preview of the document as it will appear on the page. This can be done in a number of different ways. Select **File I Print Preview** from the **Menu Bar**, click on the **Print Preview** icon 🔍 on the **Standard** Toolbar, or click on the **Preview** button on the **File I Print...** dialogue box. Whichever method you use, a new window will be displayed in Excel showing you a graphical representation of the printed page(s) as shown in Figure 5.7.

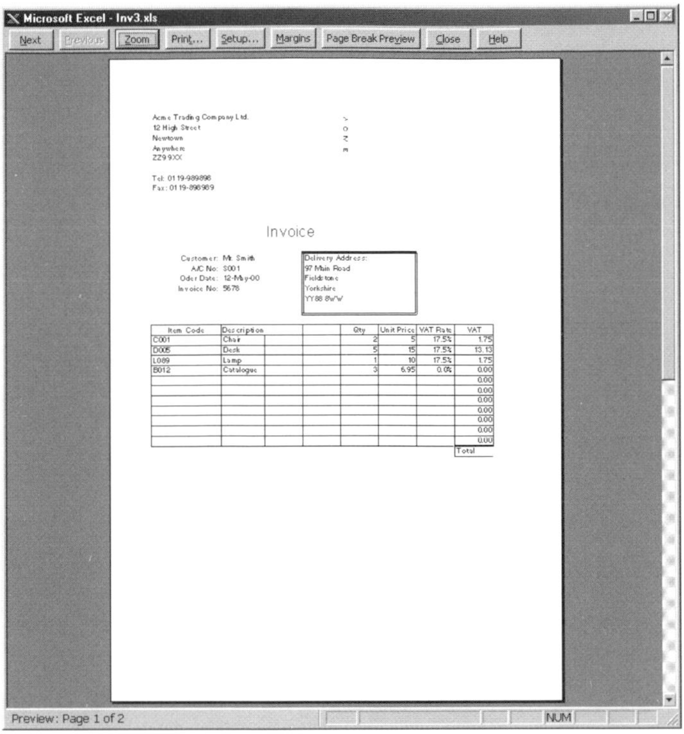

Figure 5.7 The Print Preview window.

4. The **Print Preview** window has a series of 9 control buttons running along the top as shown in Figure 5.8. Looking at these buttons from left to right the **Next** button displays the next page if the document has more than one page, whilst the **Previous** button does the opposite. The **Zoom** button allows you to magnify or shrink the page image being displayed. The **Print...** button opens the **Print** dialogue window. The **Setup...** button displays the **Page Setup** dialogue box. The **Margins** button overlays the page image with the current margin settings so you can see what the printing boundaries are and adjust the margins using the mouse. The **Page Break Preview** button is probably the most useful, as when you click on it Excel will display the current Worksheet with the page boundaries or print area shown, as in Figure 5.9. Finally the **Close** and **Help** buttons are self explanatory.

Figure 5.8 Print Preview control buttons.

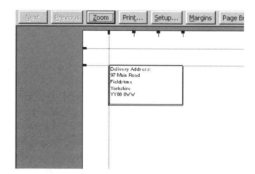

	A	B	C	D	E	F	G	H	I	J
3	Newtown									
4	Anywhere				m					
5	ZZ9 9XX									
6										
7	Tel: 0119-969898									
8	Fax: 0119-698969									
9										
10				Invoice						
11										
12	Customer:	Mr. Smith		Delivery Address:						
13	A/C No:	S001		97 Main Road						
14	Oder Date:	######		Fieldstone						
15	Invoice No:	5678		Yorkshire						
16				YY88 8WW						
17										
18										
19	Item Code	Description			Qty	Unit Price	VAT Rate	VAT	Item Total	
20	C001	Chair			2	5	17.5%	1.75	11.75	
21	D005	Desk			5	15	17.5%	13.13	88.125	
22	L089	Lamp			1	10	17.5%	1.75	11.75	
23	B012	Catalogue			3	6.95	0.0%	0.00	20.85	
24								0.00	0	
25								0.00	0	
26								0.00	0	
27								0.00	0	
28								0.00	0	
29								0.00	0	
30								0.00	0	
31								Total	####	
32										
33										

Figure 5.9 The Page Break Preview display for our Invoice.xls Worksheet.

5. Normally when printing you will need to print an entire Worksheet and when the document being printed is quite large then Excel will manage the print job and produce the relevant number of pages. However, sometimes you will only need to print a small section of a Worksheet. To do this, first select the range of cells you want to print, for example, **D12:F17** in our **Invoice.xls** Worksheet. Next, select **File I Print Area I Set Print Area** on the **Menu Bar**. This defines the area to be printed based solely on the cells selected in the Worksheet. Now, if you perform a **Print Preview** you will see that just the **Delivery Address** box on our invoice will be printed as shown in Figure 5.10.

Next	Previous	Zoom	Print...	Setup...	Margins	Page Br

Delivery Address:
97 Main Road
Fieldstone
Yorkshire
YY88 8WW

Figure 5.10 Print Preview of a selected area of our Invoice.xls Worksheet.

6. Finally, before we finish with the printing facilities in Excel, you might on occasion need to print out the actual Formulas used in a Worksheet. To do

this, first select an area of the Worksheet containing some Formulas, for
example, in our **Invoice.xls** Worksheet select the cell range **H20:I31** and
then select **Tools I Options...** on the **Menu Bar** and the tabbed dialogue
box in Figure 5.11 will be displayed. On the **View** tab make sure that the
Formulas box is ticked and then click on **OK**. The Worksheet will now
display all the Formulas. Reset the **Print Area** to the current selection and
then do a **Print Preview** which looks like the example shown in Figure 5.12.

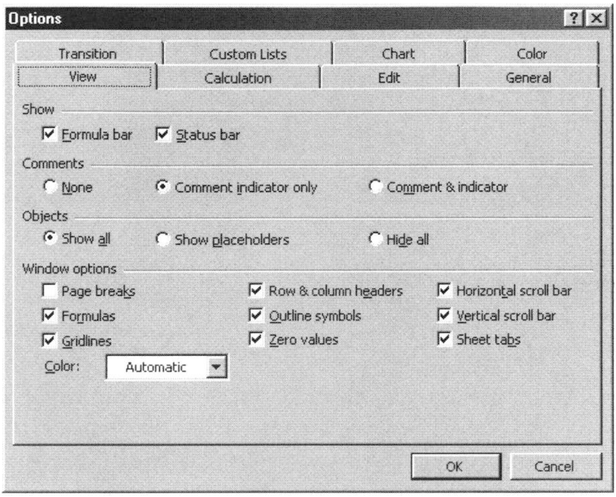

Figure 5.11 The Tools Options View tab.

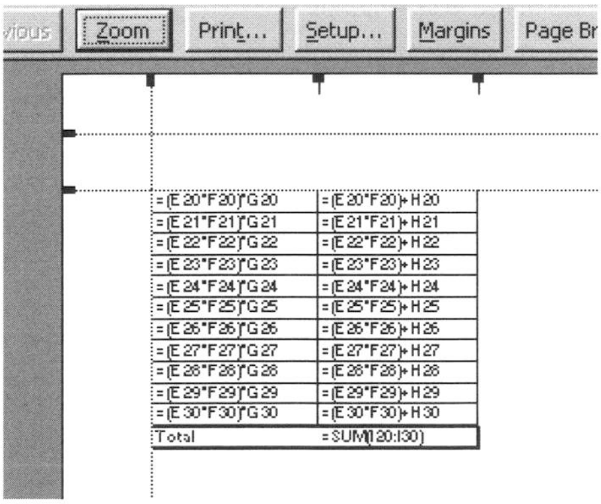

Figure 5.12 Printing Formulas Print Preview.

step **7.** **Close** the Workbook saving any changes we have made.

Summary

Printing Worksheets is pretty much an essential operation when using Excel and in this section we have learnt how we can control and manage the printing process. There are lots of things to consider, for example, the printer settings, the page settings, the print settings and even the Worksheet settings. Fortunately, the Print Preview option allows you to check everything on screen before committing anything to paper.

Review Questions

1. How can you easily ensure that any printing is centred on a page?

2. What procedure would you use to print the date on every page of a printout?

3. What Menu Bar option would you use to check how much of a Worksheet will be printed on a page?

4. You need to print just the top three rows of a particular Worksheet. How would you achieve this?

5. How can you instruct Excel to print on a particular printer?

6. You need 10 copies of your Worksheet but you don't have access to a photocopier. How can you easily produce these?

More Advanced Features

In this chapter you will learn how to

- *Import objects into a spreadsheet.*
- *Move and resize imported objects within a spreadsheet.*
- *Produce different types of charts and graphs from spreadsheet data.*
- *Edit or modify a chart or graph.*
- *Change the chart type.*
- *Move and delete charts or graphs.*

So far we have looked at the way Excel can be used to produce spreadsheets containing text, numbers, Formulas, and Functions but there are some more advanced features of the package that will allow us to be much more creative.

6.1. Importing Objects

As well as allowing us to enter various types of data into a Worksheet, Excel is capable of importing certain objects from external files.

In this section we will learn how to:

● Import objects into a spreadsheet, for example image files, graphs and text files.
● Move and resize imported objects within a spreadsheet.

Exercise 6.1

For this exercise we will use our invoice spreadsheet to see how we can add a graphical image to a Worksheet.

1. Once again, if it is not already open then **Open** the Workbook **Invoice.xls**.

2. To insert a picture on a Worksheet select **Insert I Object...** on the **Menu Bar**. This displays the **Object** dialogue box as shown in Figure 6.1. Here on the **Create New** tab you should select **Microsoft Clip Gallery** then click on **OK**.

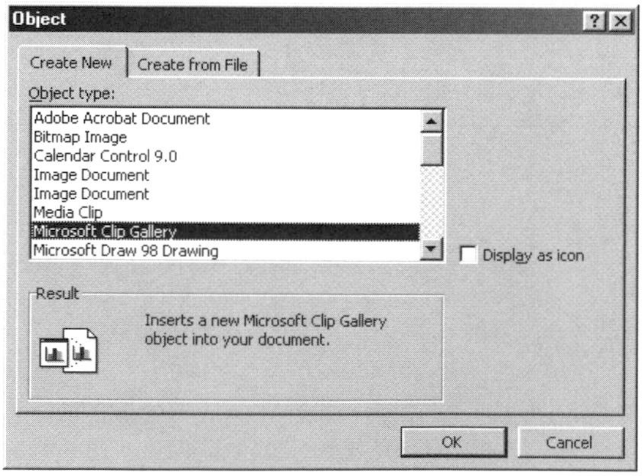

Figure 6.1 The Insert Object dialogue box.

definition

Object: An Object is any element on a Worksheet which is not contained in a cell. Objects can be created with Excel itself by, for example, using the Drawing tools.
Alternatively Objects can be 'imported' from an external source by using the Insert I Object... menu option.
Whichever method is used to incorporate an Object into a Worksheet, it is treated as a discrete element which is separate from the Worksheet but stored in the Workbook when it is saved. You can resize and move any type of Object but if an Object is imported from another file you cannot edit the contents unless you start the underlying application which was used to create it by double clicking on the Object itself.

3. A new dialogue box will appear called the **Microsoft Clip Gallery** where you can select a category by clicking on it as in Figure 6.2.

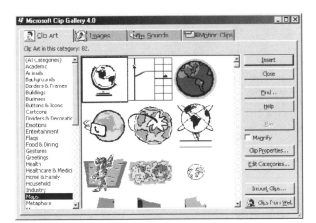

Figure 6.2 Inserting Clip Art into a Worksheet.

4. Select a likely category such as **Maps** and choose an image.

5. Once you have found a suitable image, if you click on the **Insert** button the selected image will be inserted into your Worksheet.

caution!

Depending on which version of the Microsoft Gallery has
been installed on your PC you might see a window which
is slightly different than that shown in Figure 6.2 which
applies to Gallery version 4.

 6. If your system is using Gallery version 5 you will see a dialogue box as shown
in Figure 6.3 and when you select a category you will see a new dialogue as
in Figure 6.4 from where you can select a specific image.

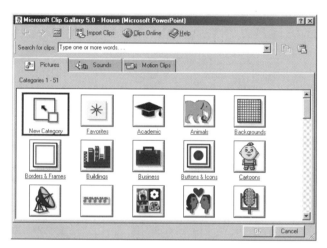

Figure 6.3 Category display in Gallery version 5.

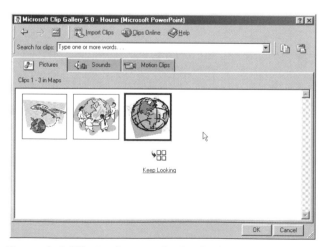

Figure 6.4 Clip Art image display in Gallery version 5.

step 7. When you select a Clip Art image in Gallery version 5 a pop up menu appears as in Figure 6.5 so that you can insert the image into your Worksheet.

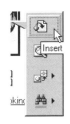

Figure 6.5 The insert image pop up menu in Gallery version 5.

step 8. Whichever version of the Microsoft Gallery you are using, the new image will appear in the centre of the Worksheet, as shown in Figure 6.6.

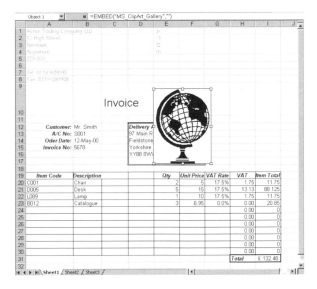

Figure 6.6 Newly inserted Clip Art images appear in the centre of a Worksheet.

step 9. Obviously having the imported picture appearing in the centre of our Worksheet is not ideal and therefore it needs to be moved to a more appropriate location. To do this you need to position the mouse pointer on the object box boundary so that the cursor changes and then click and drag the box to position it somewhere else on the Worksheet. You can also re-size the object box by dragging on the box size control handles, as in Figure 6.7.

Figure 6.7 Resizing an object.

step **10.** Use the box size control handles and the mouse pointer to resize and move the image to an appropriate position on the Worksheet. For example, as shown in Figure 6.8.

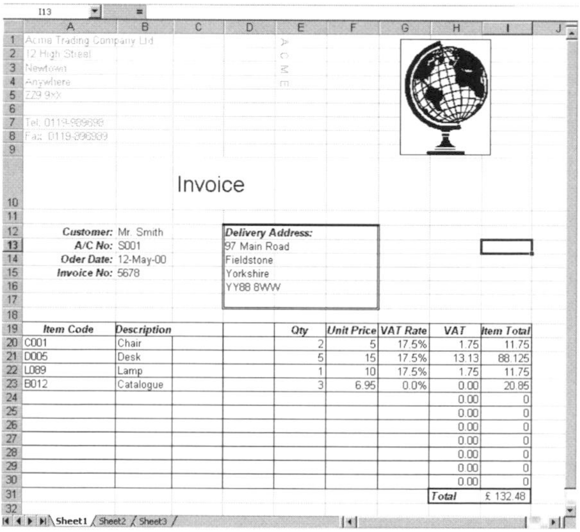

Figure 6.8 Our Invoice.xls with an image inserted.

step **11.** Finally, **Close** the Workbook saving any changes we have made.

Summary

In this section we have seen how we can incorporate external Objects, such as, Clip Art into our Worksheets. However, the example used in the exercise only demonstrates one type of Object and you should experiment with the **Insert | Object...** option to learn more about Excel's ability to use Objects.

6.2. Charts and Graphs

Typically one of the primary uses of spreadsheet packages is to process large amounts of numerical data. However, frequently analysing numbers stored in a spreadsheet can be very difficult and even taking into account Excel's powerful Formulas and Functions it can be quite daunting looking at row after row and column after column of figures.

Fortunately Excel has some excellent features for creating graphs or charts based on the data stored in Worksheets and in this section we will look at how we can:

● Produce different types of charts and graphs from spreadsheet figures to analyse data, e.g. pie charts, column charts and bar charts.
● Edit or modify a chart or graph by adding a title or label, and modifying the colours in the chart or graph.
● Change the chart type.
● Move and delete charts or graphs.

Exercise 6.2

step 1. For this exercise we will need some spreadsheet data that is suitable for analysing and turning into a graph. So, if it is not loaded then start Excel and a new blank Workbook will be created for us to work with. If Excel is already running then **Close** any open Workbooks and click on **File | New** on the **Menu Bar** or the **New** 🗋 icon on the **Standard** Toolbar.

step 2. Next, enter the following data in the specified cells:

Cell reference	Value
B2	ACME Trading Company Ltd.
B4	Monthly Sales
B6	Jan
C6	Feb
D6	Mar
E6	Apr
B7	1025
C7	998
D7	1147
E7	723

step 3. Your Worksheet should now look like the example shown in Figure 6.9.

Figure 6.9 The initial Sales.xls Worksheet.

4. Before we proceed to graph the data, **Save** the Workbook in the **My Documents** folder with the name *Sales.xls.*

Charts in Excel can be created in two different forms; as an Object embedded in a Worksheet, or as a separate 'chart' sheet within a Workbook. The procedure for creating these two types of chart is basically the same and when you use the Chart Wizard you are asked which type of chart you wish to create.

5. Creating Charts in Excel is very easy thanks to the Chart Wizard which guides you step by step through the '4 step process' of producing a chart. The first thing to do is to decide on the data that will be used to create the Chart and in our **Sales.xls** example we want to plot the sales figures for the four months. Therefore, select the cell range **B6:E7** and then select **Insert I Chart...** on the **Menu Bar**. The **Chart Wizard** will now automatically start at **Step 1** with the **Chart Type** dialogue box as shown in Figure 6.10.

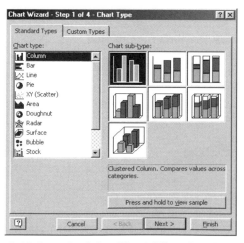

Figure 6.10 Step 1 of the Chart Wizard – choosing the chart type.

Excel is capable of creating a wide variety of different types of charts and you can select the appropriate type from Step 1 of the Chart Wizard. As well as a column chart you can create bar charts, pie charts, line charts, area charts and many others. In addition, most charts have sub types so you can for instance have a 3-D bar chart or a piec chart with the segments split up. Note that the Chart Wizard will automatically prompt you to enter the correct information that is directly relevant to the type of chart being created.

You can start the Chart Wizard by clicking on the Chart Wizard icon on the Standard Toolbar.

6. **Step 1** allows you to select both the type and the sub-type of the chart which you wish to create. For the moment we will simply accept the defaults presented i.e. a clustered column chart. Because we selected our chart data before we started the **Chart Wizard** you can use the **Press and hold to view sample** button and a preview of our chart will be displayed. Click on the **Next** button to proceed.

7. **Step 2** displays a new dialogue box called the **Chart Source Data** as shown in Figure 6.11. Here you can specify the cells where the data for the chart can be found but as we have already done this we can proceed to the next step, so click on the **Next** button to proceed.

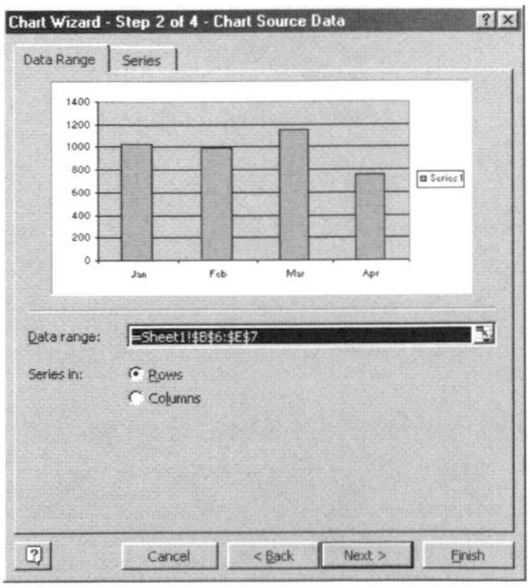

Figure 6.11 Step 2 of the Chart Wizard – selecting the data source.

8. At **Step 3** another dialogue box called the **Chart Options** is displayed as shown in Figure 6.12. This multi-tabbed dialogue box allows you to specify a whole range of chart options, such as titles, axis labels, gridlines, legends, data labels, and whether the chart should include a data table. For the moment we will ignore these options and proceed to the final step of the **Chart Wizard**. So, click on the **Next** button to proceed.

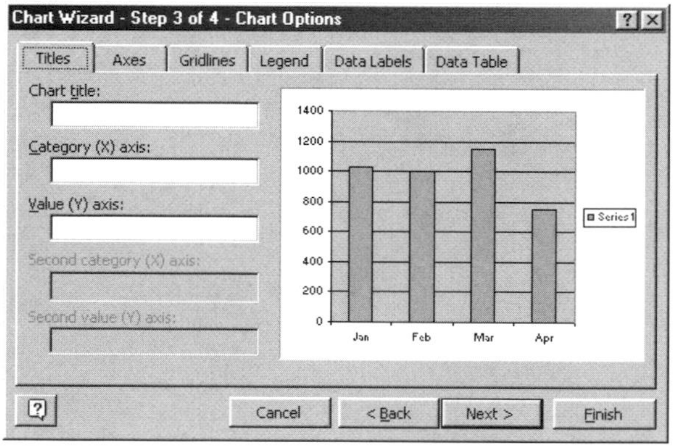

Figure 6.12 Step 3 of the Chart Wizard – specifying chart options.

9. **Step 4** displays the final dialogue box called **Chart Location**, as shown in Figure 6.13. Here we can decide whether we want the chart to be created **As new sheet:** with the sheet name **Chart1**, or **As object in:** our currently active Worksheet called **Sheet1**. In this instance we will opt for the latter, so select **As object in:** if it is not already selected and click on the **Finish** button.

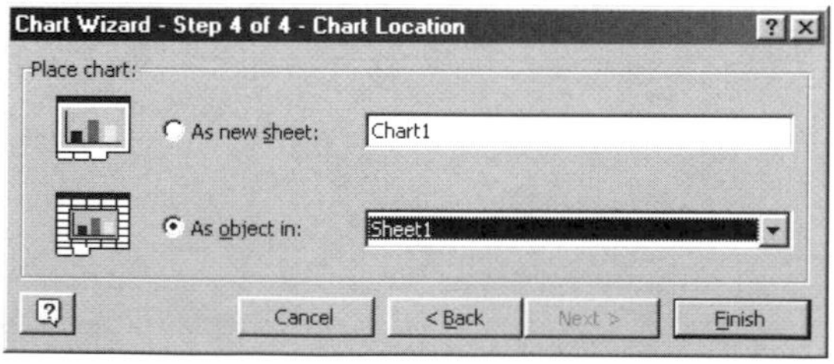

Figure 6.13 Step 4 of the Chart Wizard – deciding on the chart location.

10. As soon as you click on the **Finish** button in the **Chart Wizard** the dialogue box disappears and the newly created chart appears as an Object in the centre of your Worksheet as shown in Figure 6.14. The Chart object is already selected so you can use the box size control handles and the mouse pointer to resize and move the object to a different position on the Worksheet if you wish. Notice also that the source data range is highlighted with special coloured borders but as soon as you de-select the chart object these borders disappear.

> **Charts embedded within Worksheets are just like other Objects in that you can move and re-size them in the same way. Similarly, if you want to delete an embedded chart simply select it and press the delete key on the keyboard. The source data from which the chart was created will remain untouched.**

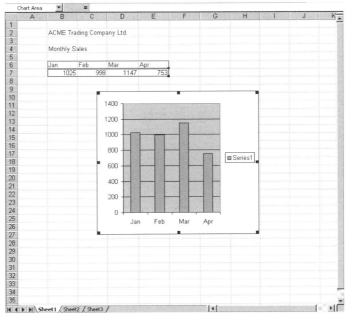

Figure 6.14 The new chart embedded as an object in our Worksheet.

step **11.** Just as Formulas change dynamically when you alter the source data, so Charts in Excel do the same. For example, on the **Sales.xls** Worksheet select cell **C7** and type in the value *200*. As soon as you press the Return or Enter key to accept the change, the chart changes to reflect the new data as shown in Figure 6.15.

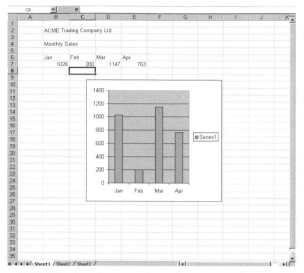

Figure 6.15 Charts change when the source data changes.

step 12. Next, select the chart on the Worksheet, then click on **Chart I Chart Options...** on the **Menu Bar**. This displays the **Chart Options** dialogue box that we originally saw in **Step 3** of the **Chart Wizard** (see Figure 6.12) and we can use this tabbed window to change various aspects of our chart. Make sure that the **Titles** tab is selected and in the **Chart title:** box type *Product Sales by Month*. In the **Category (X) axis:** box type *Month*, and in the **Value (Y) axis:** box type *Units*, as shown in Figure 6.16. You will notice that when you make these changes the chart preview window updates automatically.

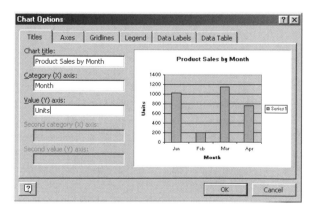

Figure 6.16 Entering the chart titles.

★ ECDL ★

13. Next, select the **Legend** tab and uncheck the **Show Legend** tick box. In the preview window the legend will disappear and the chart will re-size itself to fill the space available, as shown in Figure 6.17.

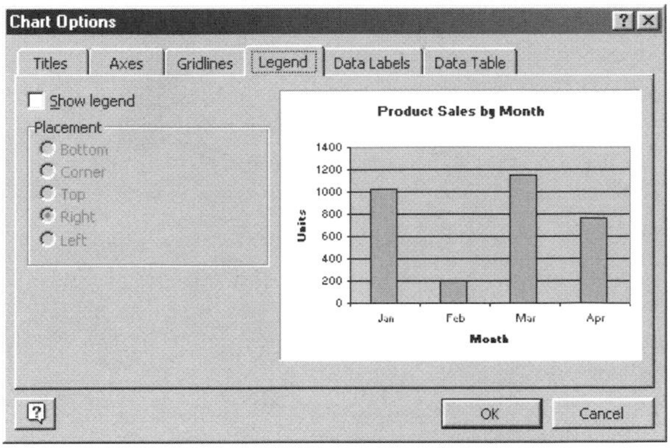

Figure 6.17 Removing the Legend.

14. Now select the **Data Labels** tab and change the **Data Labels** setting from **None** to **Show value**. In the preview window the **Unit** values will appear just above the columns on the chart, as shown in Figure 6.18.

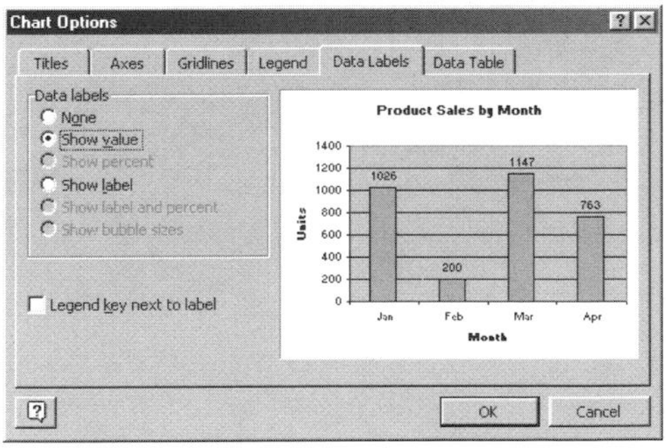

Figure 6.18 Adding the Data Labels.

15. Finally, click on the **OK** button and the **Chart Options** dialogue box will disappear leaving the chart embedded in the Worksheet updated with the changes that we have made, as shown in Figure 6.19.

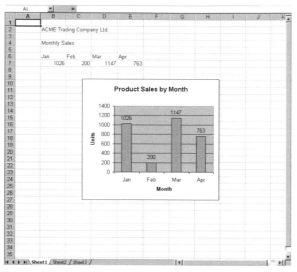

Figure 6.19 The embedded chart after changing the Chart Options.

When you re-size a chart object on a worksheet the image either shrinks or expands. Note that the scaling of the X or Y axis does not alter. If you need to rescale the axis on a chart you should select the axis and then choose **Format | Select Axis...** and using the **Scale** tab on the **Format Axis** dialog box displayed you can adjust properties of the axis such as the maximum and minimum values and the major and minor units used in the axis. In addition, you can reverse the plotting order of the values or apply a logarithmic scale if necessary.

step **16.** Before we proceed further select **File | Save** on the **Menu Bar** or click on the **Save** 💾 icon to save the changes we have made so far.

step **17.** A chart consists of many different elements, such as the plotted data series, the axes, and the data labels. Each of these elements can be formatted in their own right to change the look of a chart. For example, suppose we wanted to change the colour or shading pattern used for the columns in our Sales.xls chart. We can do this by selecting the columns with a single click with the left mouse button. Now if we select **Format | Selected Data Series...** on the **Menu Bar** a **Format Data Series** dialogue box appears, as shown in Figure 6.20.

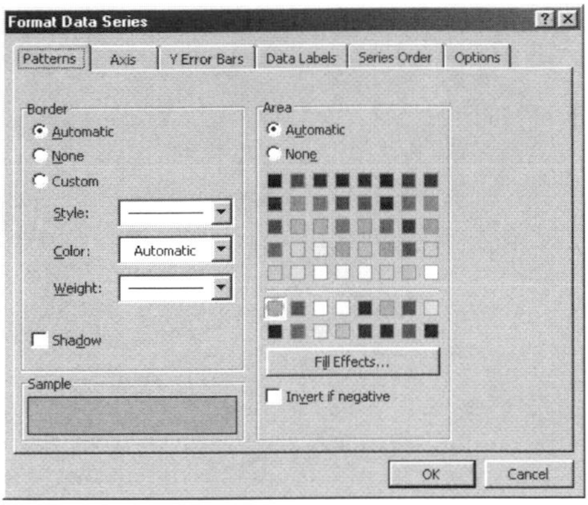

Figure 6.20 Changing the formatting of the data series.

18. On the **Patterns** tab click on the **Fill Effects...** button and a new dialogue box called **Fill Effects** will open as in Figure 6.21. Now, select the **Pattern** tab and then choose a prominent pattern to use, such as the diagonal lines, as shown in Figure 6.22.

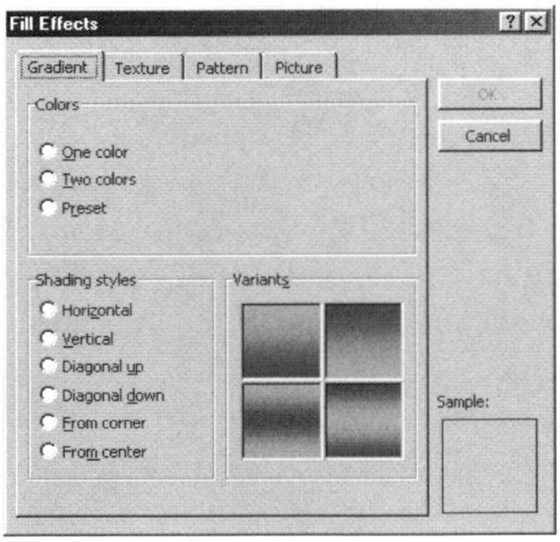

Figure 6.21 The Fill Effects window.

caution!

> Do not get confused between the Patterns tab on the Format Data Series window and the Pattern tab on the Fill Effects window, they are different. The former allows you to change the way that the borders around elements of a chart appear and the colours used, and the latter enables you to change the actual shading pattern used within a chart element such as a column or a pie slice.

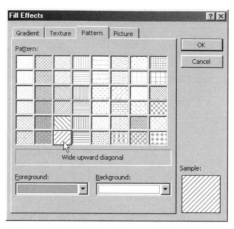

Figure 6.22 Selecting a Fill pattern.

step 19. Click on **OK** to close the **Fill Effects** window and click on **OK** to close the **Format Data Series** window. Your chart should now look similar to the example shown in Figure 6.23.

Figure 6.23 Patterned columns.

step 20. Once again, before we proceed further select **File I Save** on the **Menu Bar** or click on the **Save** 💾 icon to save the changes we have made so far.

step 21. Despite the fact that we have created a Column chart it is fairly easy to change the type of chart to something else. Select the chart object and then choose **Chart I Chart Type...** on the **Menu Bar**. This displays the **Chart Type** dialogue box that we originally saw in **Step 1** of the **Chart Wizard** (see Figure 6.10) and we can use this tabbed window to select a new type of chart to be displayed. Click on **Pie** in the **Chart type:** list and in the **Chart sub-type:** window select the top centre **3-D** sub-type, as shown in Figure 6.24.

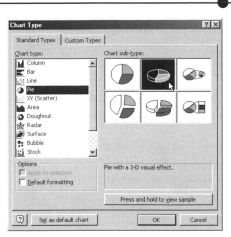

Figure 6.24 Changing the chart type.

22. In the **Options** section select the tick box labelled **Default formatting** as shown in Figure 6.25.

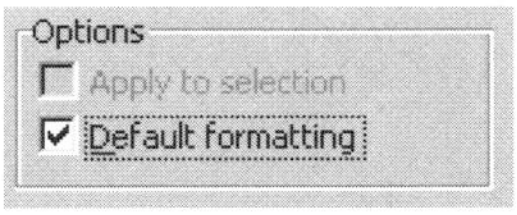

Figure 6.25 Using the default formatting for a chart.

23. Now click on the **OK** button and our embedded chart will have changed to a 3-D Pie chart like the example in Figure 6.26.

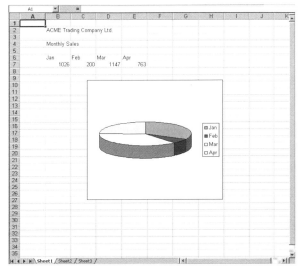

Figure 6.26 The Sales.xls chart changed into a 3-D Pie chart.

step**24.** We mentioned earlier that charts can exist as either objects on a Worksheet or as separate chart sheets within a Workbook. We can convert our embedded chart into a chart sheet by first selecting the chart object and then choosing **Chart | Location...** from the **Menu Bar**. This, if you remember, displays the **Chart Location** dialogue box that we originally saw in **Step 4** of the **Chart Wizard** (see Figure 6.13).

step**25.** When the **Chart Location** dialogue box is displayed it shows the current chart placement as an object in Sheet1. To change the location simply click on the **As new sheet:** option as shown in Figure 6.27.

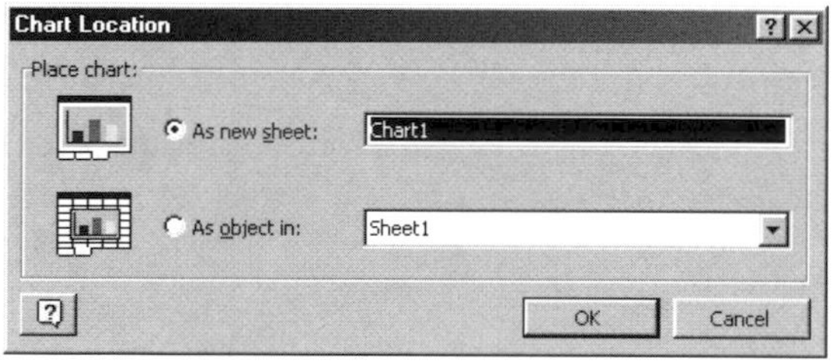

Figure 6.27 Changing the location of a chart.

step**26.** Now, when you click on the **OK** button in the **Chart Location** window the chart will switch from being an embedded object to become a separate chart sheet labelled **Chart1** within the **Sales.xls** Workbook as shown in Figure 6.28.

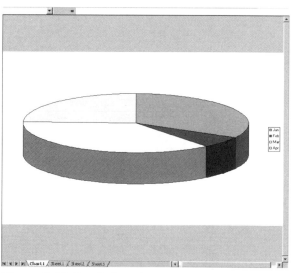

Figure 6.28 Our Sales.xls chart as a chart sheet.

step**27.** Finally, **Close** the **Sales.xls** Workbook, saving any changes made.

Summary

In this chapter we have seen how various types of chart can be generated from source data in a Worksheet. We have learnt how to format charts in lots of different ways and convert a chart from being an embedded object into a chart sheet within a Workbook. Creating charts in Excel can be very rewarding and once you start exploring the capabilities available you can produce some extremely useful results.

Review Questions

1. What is an object on a Worksheet?

2. How do you resize an object to make it smaller?

3. What happens when you double click on an object that has been inserted from another file?

4. How many Steps are there in the Excel Chart Wizard?

5. Excel charts can exist in two places. What are these two locations?

6. How do you delete an object or chart on a Worksheet?

7. Which Menu Bar options would you use to add a title to a chart?

8. How would you convert a Pie chart to a Column chart?

Final Summary

Now that you have reached the end of this guide you should have gained a good insight into the principles of using a spreadsheet application. However, this guide is not intended to be a fully comprehensive training manual for Excel 97 and there are many aspects of the package which have not been covered. Excel is the type of application that the more it is used, the more varied tasks you find it can tackle. Therefore, you are encouraged to further explore the capabilities and features of Excel in order to broaden your knowledge of the software.

If you have access to the Internet then you should start by visiting the Microsoft Excel web site where you will find plenty of additional information about the product:

http://www.microsoft.com/office/excel/default.htm

If you don't have access to the Internet, or if you are happier learning from a book, there are numerous published training guides for Excel covering every single facet of using the software.

Index

★ ECDL ★

★ ECDL ★

European Computer Driving Licence™

the european pc skills standard

Titles in the series include:

- **Module 1: Basic Concepts of Information Technology**
  ISBN: 1-85233-442-8   Softcover   £9.95

- **Module 2: Using the Computer & Managing Files**
  ISBN: 1-85233-443-6   Softcover   £9.95

- **Module 3: Word Processing**
  ISBN: 1-85233-444-4   Softcover   £9.95

- **Module 4: Spreadsheets**
  ISBN: 1-85233-445-2   Softcover   £9.95

- **Module 5: Database**
  ISBN: 1-85233-446-0   Softcover   £9.95

- **Module 6: Presentation**
  ISBN: 1-85233-447-9   Softcover   £9.95

- **Module 7: Information & Communication**
  ISBN: 1-85233-448-7   Softcover   £9.95

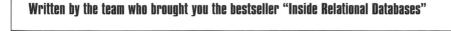
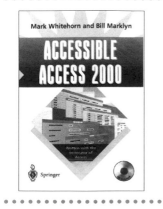